# A FIELD GUIDE

# TO IMPOSSIBLE MEN

Merry
Christmas 88
Lori

# A
# FIELD
# GUIDE
# TO
# IMPOSSIBLE
# MEN

Linda Stasi

ST. MARTIN'S PRESS • NEW YORK

*For*
Kevin Dornan
*and*
Stuart Spikerman:

*Completely Impossible!*

*Illustrations by Lizzy Rockwell*

A FIELD GUIDE TO IMPOSSIBLE MEN
Copyright © 1987 by Linda Stasi. All rights reserved. Printed in the United States of America. No part of this book may be used or reproduced in any manner whatsoever without written permission except in the case of brief quotations embodied in critical articles or reviews. For information, address St. Martin's Press, 175 Fifth Avenue, New York, N.Y. 10010.

*Library of Congress Cataloging-in-Publication Data*

Stasi, Linda.
 A field guide to impossible men.

 1. Men—Anecdotes, facetiae, satire, etc.
2. American wit and humor.   I. Title.
PN6231.M45S72   1987     818'.5402      87-16367
ISBN 0-312-00990-9 (pbk.)

First Edition

10  9  8  7  6  5  4  3  2  1

# Contents

**PART TWO:**
Impossible Lovers,
Mothers, & Others

# Acknowledgments
# Thank You

Toni Lopopolo, my editor, for taking this book on. Julie Coopersmith for taking this book on. Amy Gottlieb for helping in the design. My daughter, Jessica, and my mother, Florence, for just being funny. And thank you, too, to all my friends and family for supplying stories, anecdotes, and trivia that I relished.

# Introduction

## So, You've Got an Impossible (Dream) Man . . .

Everything seemed so right. He was all the things you thought you were looking for . . . good-looking, smart, sexy. Unfortunately he was also impossible to live with, talk to, and have a normal relationship with. Every woman who is alive and breathing has dated, mated, and/or (God forbid!) married one Impossible Dream Man or another in her time. You may in fact have one hanging around in your life right now. How can you tell?

Impossible Dream Men are the guys who never call back after the best date you've ever had in your whole life, or worse, they never stop calling after the worst one you've ever had.

Many women foolishly get the impression after they've successfully extricated themselves from one Impossible Dream Man that they will be able to spot the next one who comes along from a hundred yards. Wrong. What they don't realize is that there are millions of them . . . disguised in ways you simply can't imagine.

For example, have you ever been with a man who exhibits any of the following bizarre behaviors?

- Asks you to go away with him on your first date?

- Calls after a six-month absence and acts like he saw you yesterday?

- Buys you a balloon, or worse, wants to fly a kite with you?

- Seems to be having a religious experience when describing his cleaning lady?

- Freely admits to an open fear of sushi?

- Swears he hung around with Mother Teresa, he's so good?

- Claims he's never done this sort of thing before?

- Tells you of his plans for his next vacation . . . a year in advance?

- Gives you the distinct impression that he knows hundreds of models with no cellulite?

- Asks you how much rent you pay? (*Before* he asks you out!)

- Swears that he and his wife have separate beds . . . or that they live like strangers?

- Makes you feel like being with him is like having a ringside seat at Lourdes?

If any of the above rings true, you (check one):

1. have   2. had   3. are about to have   4. have been had by   5. can't get rid of   6. have been cleared of all charges in the murder of . . . an Impossible Dream Man.

This book is designed to help you. After all, Murder One is a serious charge.

# PART ONE

Everything
You Need to Know
About
Every Kind
of
Impossible Man!

## The Golden Rules

1. Be careful what you wish for. You might get it.

2. Be sure to include what you *don't* want in that wish, as well. (Otherwise, it's bound to be thrown in for the hell of it.)

3. If you ignore rule number two, you automatically lose your right to complain if that incredibly smart, sexy, successful rich hunk who would marry you in a second needs to stick M&M's up his nose while singing "Twist and Shout" before he can make love.

4. Be careful what you wish for. You might get it.

**IMPOSSIBLE MAN #1**

# Mogul in His Own Time
## (AKA: Desperado)

Mogul is among the most appealing of Impossible Men. He is also, without doubt, the most flamboyant and the most unpredictable, in everything but his mating habits. But there are certain distinct characteristics that make it possible to spot him . . . and then to beat him at his own game . . . if you've got nerves of steel, an ego as big as Montana, and no thighs to speak of. And even though that eliminates everyone who isn't under contract to Eileen Ford, let's proceed. The man you love may be a Mogul.

Mogul calls the world his own, which means that Mogul does not work for anyone but himself, and for himself he works like a dog. He often lives in several places, which are usually the best of places. In fact, Mogul should be a boutique, so that he can have shopping bags that would have "MOGUL: NEW YORK, DENVER, MILANO" (or wherever) printed across them.

Mogul makes and spends money. Lots of money. On himself and on the people who might someday help to make him rich(er). And never forget that he does what he does (or did what he did), for a living just so that he could become a mogul. He can be a doctor mogul (surgeon, not a proctologist or an orthodontist), a lawyer mogul (divorce—*maybe* taxes—never civil liberties), an entrepreneur (microchips, not ladies half-size dresses), maybe a restaurateur (to the stars, not their fans). He is also attracted to fields of entertainment, and sometimes publishing, which he will get "into" after he's made his millions in microchips. He will often get into entertainment by putting up millions of other people's dollars to become a producer. This, of course, affords him the opportunity of "taking a meeting" with Steven Spielberg, Billy Joel, and Martin Scorcese (all of whom are perfect examples of the breed).

If Mogul gets into publishing, he will eventually own the company and sell the rights to his book, *Mogul in His Own Time,* to another house. (He wants the biggest advance money, and he's not known to be generous with his authors.)

What does all of this mean in real life? It means that Mogul simply cannot have co-workers who are peers because they would see through him and cause an office insurrection that would make the Crusades look like a piece of cake in comparison. What would they see? They'd see that he's all grease and no machinery. Therefore, to avoid this uncomfortable situation, he engineers it so that he is *always* head of the hive, which gives him the most loyal followers, and that includes male drones (stingless workers) and female queens.

## What You See . . . and What You Get

Right off the bat you notice that Mogul likes beautiful women. Many beautiful women. Mogul is never seen with a dog, unless her pedigree is so long that it includes two signers of the Declaration of Independence and some Euro-royalty (it's okay if it's shaky). The woman or (precisely) women he marries are never very clever or witty, or at least they are smart enough to not let on if they are.

Mogul is proud that he is no gentleman, even though he owns two hand-tailored tuxedos and can wield a fish knife with the best of them. He has a dangerous air about him, but you don't know why.

Mogul has not attended the very best schools, but they really weren't all that bad, either . . . and he likes to give the impression that he clawed his way to the top from the streets. Unfortunately they were tree-lined streets filled with nice, middle-class suburban people. But since this looks rotten on the résumé of life, he tends to ignore it.

Can you imagine the humiliation he'd suffer if his real background were ever discovered and his Little League coach was interviewed for *People* magazine? So, Mogul will go to great lengths to keep his background a secret, which gives him the double advantage of sounding even more mysterious. Of course, if you are friendly with Mogul he will not fail to hint to you how hard his parents struggled to make ends meet. While you are picturing a cold-water flat, he's talking about the time they took out a loan to add a dormer.

9

Mogul has cultivated a manner of speech that is neither city nor country. You could call it tough-guy announcer for want of a better word. He very rarely allows any regional background nasal sounds to pass through unless he can use it to his advantage. If he comes from New England, he pronounces his *r*'s like a midwesterner, and if he comes from the south, he only sounds like a good ol' boy when gambling. This of course gives him an advantage in a high-stakes game with big-time easterners who think he's a country boy. They think that, until he walks away with the pot.

## Foreground

Mogul has three patterns of behavior, which he uses in all situations. They are:

1) inconsiderate 2) irresponsible 3) irresistible.

He will use all three on you at once, but you will only notice the irresistible part. In fact, you won't notice numbers one and two until it is, regrettably, too late. So don't take it personally if you are suddenly assaulted with what you consider a grave injustice from someone who claimed to love and adore you. He doesn't consider it an injustice at all . . . in fact, he considers it true justice: equal treatment for all. And it's as easy as one, two, three!

The question of why Mogul is driven the way he is remains a mystery. Those who have given birth to and reared Moguls in Their Own Time claim it has something to do with too much Kraft macaroni and cheese at an early age. Psychiatrists scoff at this notion and say that this is simply a poor excuse and a perfect example of mother-guilt transference.

## Mogul and His Nasty, Nasty, Past

For whatever reason, an air of danger seems to surround this charmer. Well, fortunately or unfortunately, the whole thing has no basis in reality, unless you count the one time (while he was still in college) that he got arrested for selling pot and spent the better part of an hour in jail.

He now belongs to the finest private clubs, wears hand-tailored clothing, and has had the good sense to save the jeans he wore in the tenth grade. He often wears these jeans with a tweed jacket to the office. You will never see Mogul less than impeccably turned out. His taste is suberb and in fact . . .

## You Wouldn't Catch Him Dead Wearing:

1. **Gold chains:** His stainless Rolex and beat-up old Bulova and/or Timex are all the jewelry he owns or ever cares to own. No one knows whatever became of all of the jewelry all of the women in his life have tried to impose upon him for birthdays and various religious holidays. Suffice it to say that these no longer seem to exist, for whatever reason.

2. **Fur coats or other attention-grabbing outerwear:** His Burberry does very well for most occasions, thank you very much. When he goes formal, there is a cashmere topcoat, and when he's wearing jeans—which is most of the time—he's got these jackets that he wears and they're probably either tweed or from L. L. Bean.

3. **Designer jeans:** Levi's and Wranglers were good enough in high school and they're good enough now. And as for women . . .

11

## He Wouldn't Be Caught Dating:

1. **Women with too much jewelry:** Too much is anything given you by someone else and/or wearing more than one piece at a time that he's given you.

2. **Women who would wear Candies outside the bedroom:** He's the first one to admit that he doesn't mind getting heeled in the bedroom by a mule, but he'll be damned if anyone's gonna know about it!

3. **Sissy women:** If you can't ride a horse, swim a mile, and drive more recklessly than he, either forget it or sign up for some lessons. Fast!

4. **Naggy, whiny women:** Remember, complaining is *not* the same as whining. Complaining gracefully (he thinks) is very Palm Beach. And that's good. Whining, on the other hand (he thinks), is very Miami Beach. And that's bad. So in other words, you can complain that the wine is not vintage, but you can't complain that the piña colada tastes like feet. Got it?

5. Suzanne Somers

## Women He Would Die to Date

- Women who are tall, blond, gorgeous, and have been featured in *Vogue* on any page other than the back-of-the-book hemorrhoid ads.

- Women who are recognized in any Gucci store anywhere in the world . . . *before* they show their American Express card.

- Cheryl Tiegs, or anyone once married to John Derek.

## How to Mate a Mogul

Mogul will begin each romance with great flourish, even though it is, again, nothing personal. He must have what he wants, and he has found ways of getting it every time.

It goes something like this: He sees you and decides right on the spot that you are too upscale for him. You just need to have a certain air about you that makes him feel dull and suburban. He will then take you to the very best restaurant, where the head waiter knows him . . . of course. He looks deeply into your eyes, smiles with a sexual bravado that makes you believe not only that you're utterly charming but that he knows more about you than you'd care to reveal. That one look has been known to cause even the smartest of women to believe that she's got him locked up tight. Wrong. Even though he seems like he's smitten (genuinely, honestly, you *know* when a guy's a goner), he's just flirting. (Believe me; it's true.)

During dinner he will take your hand, hold it in his, and look at it with wonder before he kisses your palm. He will then look back and say something very dirty, knowing full well that no one has ever had the nerve to talk dirty to you before (at least not during dinner). Not only has he chosen you to have dinner with, he wants you—*and* he talks dirty. Oh, boy!

Let's take a look at a bit of the conversation:

## His Way

WHAT HE SAYS:    I want to take you to my house in Haiti and make love to you for days on end. You're an incredible woman, and I'm having the most incredible fan-

|  |  |
|---|---|
| | tasies of what I want to do to you. |
| WHAT HE MEANS: | So, do I get lucky tonight or what? |
| WHAT SHE SAYS: | But I hardly know you! You're making me blush! |
| WHAT SHE MEANS: | Is he for real? Or is this the old seduce-and-abandon routine? |
| WHAT HE SAYS: | I do know you, and I want to know you better. |
| WHAT HE MEANS: | This is a snap, she'll be sending me cute cards before the week is out. |
| WHAT SHE SAYS: | Well, I want to know you better too. |
| WHAT SHE MEANS: | I want to marry you next week. |

Obviously, you are managing to have two different conversations at the same time. You're planning the wedding, and he's planning to score. And you're all wrong. One simply cannot deal with Mogul as though he were a decent and honorable human being. He isn't, and he has no intention of ever becoming any such thing. Don't even get excited if Mogul tells you that he's falling in love with you on your first date. Remember, it's nothing personal. So, please note and do it . . .

## Your Way

| | |
|---|---|
| HE SAYS: | I want to take you to my house, my house in Haiti, and make love to you for days on end. You're an . . . |

SHE SAYS: . . . incredible woman and I'm having the most incredible fantasies of what I want to do to you.

HE SAYS: Huh?

SHE SAYS: Dudley Moore in *Ten*, right?

This is all well and good, but keep in mind that at some point, even though you are playing it cool, he will still switch tactics on you and act as though he is completely annoyed by you and by your behavior. He will ignore you and even get nasty. This is the point when even the best have crumbled. Don't even notice. Let him think that you care so little that his change of heart went completely unnoticed by you. It will make him even nutsier.

But do dole out little niceties that you don't mean. If he says he loves you, say: "And in my way, I love you too." If he tells you he wants to marry you, don't plan a big wedding; marry him immediately and call your parents later. But remember, he will never marry you if you are too good in bed, because he must worry about pleasing you to be really pleased himself.

Oddly, he will actually settle in very nicely after the wedding as long as you don't become too involved in his existence. If you become the adoring "other half," he will take up with a model-turned-actress who is gorgeous and is trying to find herself. So spend an inordinate amount of time worrying about *your* career, *your* publishing debut, *your* problems. If you worry too much about his well-being, he'll make your life hell. Remember, with Mogul, no good deed goes unpunished. He must work for sex and love the way he works at everything else, or he feels cheated. Keep him working overtime to win you at all times, and he's yours for life.

Now what about children? Does Mogul like

them? You bet. As long as they can play a good game of squash, he'll adore them. And chances are good that they'll play a hell of a game of squash, because they are *his* kids after all. Now, here's something that you may not have thought of: Mogul's children will be an awful lot like him, so you've got to work really hard to keep them from selling teacher-indulgences and bathroom time to the other tots at nursery school. Aside from that, look the other way a lot, and he's yours for life.

Be careful what you wish for . . . you might just get it!

## BEST OF BREED

### Moguls in Their Own Time

Most Likely to Keep Succeeding:
BILLY JOEL

MICK JAGGER

Best Performance by an Actor
in an Old Role:
DONALD TRUMP

Best Performance by a Female
Impersonator:
LEONA HELMSLEY

Who Even Cares?
MESHOLEM RIKLIS*

*(Best known outside his plane as "What's his name,
that guy who married what's her name, Pia Zadora?")

**IMPOSSIBLE MAN #2**

# Jock-Eek!

Jock is the most pleasant-seeming of all impossible men for the simple reason that he seems like such a regular guy. And he *is* a regular guy. You will never catch him saying things like "joie de vivre" or "fabulous," because those aren't the kinds of things that people yell at the World Series.

Which brings us to point number one. Jock's life revolves around ball games of all sorts. If God had meant him to enjoy sensitive dinner parties with your friends, he wouldn't have invented the sphere. In fact when quizzed on what he believes is the greatest invention of all time, he would probably answer the air pump.

Jock spends at least 60 percent of his time playing sports, thinking about sports, watching sports, or finding new and unusual ways to participate in sports. Some of these include:

- Venturing into the worst neighborhoods imaginable to join the pickup basketball game in the junior high school yard.

- Hanging out in Herman's till closing time discussing the best ways to get a racquet restrung.

- Starting a football pool in his office.

- Bribing the folks at Ticketron before the season even starts. (There's always a season and always a play-off.)

- Running the marathon.

- Training for the marathon. (There's always a marathon.)

## Where He Came From

To know him you've got to know his background. His parents could have been Ozzie and Harriet. He spent his entire childhood throwing the ball around with Dad, while Mom baked cookies for her "men."

He was a high school football, baseball, lacrosse, swimming, and tennis champ, and he had a million friends. He still does. They were always around then, and they are always around now.

He grew up in a nice suburban neighborhood and there was a miniature football waiting for him in his bassinet when he arrived home from the hospital. As he grew, he began

19

to understand many of the questions of the universe such as why a football field is a certain length, and that somehow no matter how many kids came by on any given day, his room stayed neat (even if *their* rooms were frightening).

If at all possible, you should try to visit his parents' home, just to get a look at the room that was. Chances are better than good it will still look like the Baseball Hall of Fame. What strikes you most of all is the order. You will find banners up at jaunty angles on the wall, there will be the desk made of shelves with a covered plywood top with a pencil cup filled with sharpened pencils, and plenty of Bic pens. You might even to your horror discover a book open on the desk to a watercolor of Mickey Mantle. There will be the maple boy-bed and the plaid bedspread. It looks like you just stepped back in time, and obviously no one thinks that it is unusual to keep his old room this way. Perhaps Mom hopes that he'll be back after track practice. Who knows?

## Where He Is Now

You might meet him at a local pub, or through your work. You have a better than even chance of meeting him at work if you happen to be a teacher, because even if he isn't the gym teacher in your school, he'll show up there sooner or later to use the track.

He lives in an apartment that looks like his college dorm gone berserk. He isn't ashamed to bring you there, although God knows he should be. The place would give the Collier brothers a nervous breakdown. And he can't figure out why it's such a mess. It upsets him that his bed has a wet towel on it from the morning (thank God he does most of his showering in locker rooms or his entire apartment would be encased in fog from all the wet towels he'd leave around). He worries that last night's take-out Chinese food has taken on a life of its own in its paper container on the couch. He whines that he has to keep buying underwear and socks because he never seems to have any clean ones unless his mother pays a visit and does the wash.

## Your First Date

On your first date you will notice that he speaks in sports tongues you can't follow. When talking about friends, you'll need a dictionary. For example:

WHEN HE SAYS: He scored.

HE MEANS: He got laid; he bought coke; or he made a good real estate deal.

WHEN HE SAYS: She scored.

HE MEANS: She got *him* into bed.

WHEN HE SAYS: He's got the whole nine yards.

HE MEANS: Someone with a new car, a great apartment, and season tickets to pro football.

WHEN HE SAYS: She's got the whole nine yards.

HE MEANS: A woman who got the new car, the great apartment *and* the season tickets in the divorce settlement. He may be referring to his ex-wife.

WHEN HE SAYS: I've got sports channel. Wanna watch the hockey game with me Tuesday?

HE MEANS: Do you fool around?

21

## The Look of Him . . .
## The Lure of You

Jock-Eeks the world over look exactly the same, with the exception of Italian soccer players who drape their jackets over their shoulders and hold cigarettes the way Nazis did in World War II movies.

## His Wardrobe:
## If Clothes Make the Man,
## He Should Commit Suicide

Now if you've hit upon a jock who isn't an Italian soccer player, you'll notice (or ignore completely) his nice but somewhat boring wardrobe. Chances are good that he has the same brown or khaki corduroy sports jacket and collection of light-blue button-down broadcloth shirts that he's had since college. He also has the biggest collection of Izod shirts in town and owns gym shorts in every conceivable condition. Rounding off the collection are several pairs of jeans without designer tags, one pair of gray flannel slacks, and a couple of pair of khakis. He thinks of these things as a wardrobe.

You'll notice that his entire "wardrobe" consists of Christmas presents and things one can purchase at Herman's. Since the only kind of suit one can purchase at Herman's is made of sweatshirt material, it can get pretty tough to take him out to black tie and semiformal parties. So, while he won't *expect* you to buy his clothes for him, if you don't he will show up at your best friend's wedding in his corduroy sports jacket and topsiders. (He thinks they're formal shoes because they are brown and don't have Adidas written on the side.)

He also:

- Wears only jockey briefs.

- Has many baseball hats, but favors one in particular.

- Sometimes inexplicably ventures out of the house wearing gym shorts over sweat pants.

- Has never to your knowledge owned a pair of black socks or shoes.

### What He Drapes Those Clothes on Is Another Story Altogether: The Jock and His Body: The Deadly Duo

Let's face it, his body makes you weak in the knees, elbows, upper body, and everywhere else you can think of. He's got a real man's body, and you love just looking at it. There's substance to it. It has a lot of squared off stuff that's different from anything you have. In fact, it's even different stuff than most other men have. And while you pretend that it's all kinds of other things that you love about him, it's really that he makes you want to take large bites out of him.

He's in good shape even if he's got a slight pot from too much Miller Lite and food served from neck trays at one too many stadiums. But who cares, when he's got legs and shoulders like that? They don't have to be huge shoulders, they just have to be strong shoulders.

He usually has a conservative haircut and he wouldn't dream of changing the style or having it cut anywhere but by the same person he's been going to since he hit town. His first manicure comes *after* he's dead. All in all, a macho package that you're shocked to be so attracted to after you swore that men who didn't enjoy

23

the same things that you do were not worth your time. After a month with him you're probably saying things about quality versus quantity time and hanging out at Ticketron so that you just "might run into him by mistake." Ask your mother to make a novena that the toots at the ticket booth doesn't tell him you've been there for seventy-two hours. If only you could spend some "quantity" time with him, you'd run for the hills in about three days, but until he's ready to settle down, his very elusiveness makes him irresistible . . . but . . .

## When a Jock Catches Wife-o-Mania Watch Out!

There comes a time in every Jock-Eek's life when he must come to grips with the fact that his entire apartment is out of control. There is simply no order and he can't figure out why last year's *Sports Illustrated*s are all piled up on the couch and at the foot of his bed. Why hasn't every one except the swimsuit edition been tossed out? Then it hits him! Marriage was invented for this very purpose! When there is a wife, there is order.

Wasn't his parents' house always neat? His parents couch never crunched from potato chip crumbs when you sat on it. When he sits on his couch, it sounds like a one-man band. He can never even remember when he found a wet towel on his bed at home. When he decides that a wife is what's needed to straighten out this mess, be careful . . . the life he picks may be your own.

Now don't get all excited, even if you *do* have an out of control crush on him. It's nothing personal. It's just that it took him this many years to figure out why men get married: It's so that they don't have to sit in potato chip crumbs.

So, if for some reason better known only to yourself and God, you decide that you will die if you don't have him to call your own, then you must know up front that to win him all you need do is be completely organized in your home, and be around when Wife-o-Mania strikes.

You should also know that you will *never* be as important as a play-off game of any kind at any time, and certainly never as important as the . . . ummm . . . pregame *schedule*. It cannot change, and you cannot whine it, will it, or force it to. It generally goes something like this:

## Wide World of Sports: A Day-by-Day Calendar of Events

*Monday:* Monday night football. Either it will be watched at the local pub with all his friends, or it will be watched in your living room with all his friends. They expect beer, chips, and to be left alone to male-bond.

*Tuesday:* Racquet ball or tennis till about 10:30 at night.

*Wednesday:* (From 7:00 P.M. till . . .) "Pickup" basketball game at the junior high, weather permitting. (That means games are not played during hurricanes and temperatures below $-20°$.) Games are over much too late for grown men to be hanging around terrible neighborhoods, so each week you get sick to your stomach thinking that he's been killed. What you don't know is that half of his team mates are convicted felons and are so busy playing basketball that they don't have time to steal, mug, and rape. He and some of his friends are too old to be playing this hard, which also makes you sick with fear. All you know is that once one of them collapsed, and he and the convicted felons were shocked when the guy didn't show the following Wednesday night. They didn't exactly call him a fairy but they secretly thought it.

*Thursday Night:* Season hockey, basketball, baseball, etc., tickets.

*Friday:* Yours, all yours. He will take you to a movie and out to dinner. It is also the night that you act like a couple and go out with other couples. (His friends and their girlfriends most likely.)

*Saturday:* Tennis or softball with his friends in the morning and afternoon. The late afternoon is the only time to grab him if you want him to go shopping with you.

*Sunday:* Golf with his father unless it's football season, in which case you can count on a living room full of guys screaming. It is only *after* you run *out* screaming yourself that you realize that all that cheering all those years in the background of your life was not for you and your martyrdom of Sunday afternoons.

### How to Know when Wife-o-Mania Is About to Strike

- He willingly goes to your male friend's dinner party and not *once* says that any guy who has china is a fairy.

- He gives up a Sunday football game to go to your neice's graduation party. (He runs into a bedroom with a TV and closes the door to watch the game in secret, but at least he's showed up.)

- He takes you to Herman's and buys you a handball glove. He does this the way normal men buy you flowers.

- He asks you out for the weekend *without* calling Ticketron first.

- He asks you if you've ever gotten into bed only to discover a wet towel that you left there that morning.

### How to Know
### if You Are About to Succumb
### to Wife-o-Mania

- You refrain from saying that any sport where men wear Calypso pants and hit each other on the behind while huddling seems blatantly latent.

- You know a punt from a kick.

- You care that you know.

- You and your mother ask the salesmen at Herman's if they have a bridal registry.

- You know the number of Sportsline by heart.

- You love your new handball glove.

### Life as the Wife

Now I realize that life with this one doesn't seem too bad. After all, he does have a great sense of humor and he likes to have fun. Granted, most of the fun has to do with some sort of competitive game that doesn't include you, but . . .

What you won't realize going into this is that Jock likes tradition, which means that now that he's grown up he should have an Ozzie and Harriet life too. Therefore, he figures, no matter how much the guys horse around, things will always be returned to order. I don't know whether he exactly expects you to do it, but he'll be real upset if it isn't done. He'll also expect you to be "independent."

**in·de·pen·dent** *(in-di-'pen-dent), adj. 1. the ability to let him go where and when he wants whenever he wants without getting upset or jealous and without ever wanting to do the same with your friends.*

Well, if all this is okay with you and you think that you can deal with this and proceed as the happy newlyweds, that's fine. But even if you have the patience of Job as a wife, chances are good that unless you were a wife in 1950, you will want to kill him when you have kids. Even then he thinks that he can leave you night after night to play some game or—worse—bring a bunch of his screaming potato-chip-throwing friends over to watch the game. (It doesn't matter which, just that there always *is* one!) You'll want to tie the laces of his sneakers together every time he gets that gym-bag look in his eye.

He'll also expect you to be great at being wifey. In exchange for your services, he will accompany you to the symphony or the ballet from time to time and make fun of the male dancers in tights. When you mention that football players wear similar tights, he will get mad and you will have a fight, but he will enjoy retelling the story time and time again.

As a lover, he can be fun because it's such athletic sex. No kidding. And as long as you can keep it more of a clinch than a huddle, it can be really good. He's completely uninhibited and makes you that way too.

*What he's not:* Experimental. Anything that smacks of the exotic makes him nervous. So without proper coaxing, he can become McLover. So unless you want a sign over your bed that says 3 billion served . . . lukewarm, be prepared to teach him some new tricks. And be prepared to have him pale at the suggestions. What kind of men would do *that*!? he wonders. Then when you get *him* to do *that*, he worries that he's becoming weird and (God forbid!) a deviant.

*What he's really not:* Concerned about what you really want. He assumes that you are having as good a time as he is, so it always comes as a shock to him that you'd even think of doing something like *that!*

## Jock as Dad

Jock makes a great father unless his children (particularly his sons) happen to be more interested in arts and crafts than playing some sort of sports. He will teach his daughters to pitch and shoot baskets, drive golf balls, and hit homers as easily as he teaches his sons. What he will be with his daughters is fair. What he will be with you is chauvinistic. He will even be this way if you are more of a jock than he. But jocks don't tend to marry jocks as often as they marry model-types the first go 'round. Second marriages are something else again. He may treat his second wife with the same sense of fair play that he treats his daughters.

The only fly in the ointment here is that Jock can't stand playing with anyone who isn't as good as he is, so he expects his kids to learn to compete with him as soon as they are out of diapers. And chances are good that they will. They'll adore him and expect you to go along with it all and somehow not have everything a mess. You may have to sell them at birth.

## BEST OF BREED

### Jock-Eek!

When Jocks Go Bad:
First Place:
JOE PEPITONE
for keeping the blond wife
no matter what the jury says

Second Place:
JOE NAMATH
for keeping the blond wife no matter
how many pairs of panty hose he owns

Third Place:
JIM BROWN
for keeping his blond girlfriends
no matter what the press said about
all the other blond girlfriends

The Men Who Found a Way
to Make Even More Women
Lust After Them After They Stopped
Chasing Balls Around Fields:
HUEY LEWIS

JULIO IGLESIAS

No One Has Ever in the History of
the World Ever Looked Better in
Underwear:
JIM PALMER

Best Celluloid Heroes
WILLIAM BENDIX
in *The Babe Ruth Story*

GARY COOPER
in *The Lou Gehrig Story*

JAMES CAAN
in *Brian's Song* (and any other time)

**IMPOSSIBLE MAN #3**

# The Disaster Master

The Disaster Master is a mess, and it's a wonder that any women like him at all, let alone make a conscious effort to actually go after him. Some women wrongly believe, however, that there is a shortage of men. The truth of the matter is that when the pollsters counted eligible men, they discounted the Disaster Master. They figured he'd be dead by the time the poll was published.

Why is he a disaster? For one thing, he is always falling prey to what he considers a major life-threatening calamity or illness. If he sneezes, he says, "God damn, I'm catching the flu." If you sneeze, he says, "Weren't you taught to carry Kleenex?" Nothing is unimportant

31

when it comes to his health, his phobias, his wallet. He'll spend an inordinate amount on doctors, but not—I repeat, *not*—on dinner.

He is a fanatic about food and cleanliness . . . yours and his. He's allergic to dust, pollen, cigarette smoke, perfume, and red dye numbers 1, 2, 3, 4, 5, 6, 7, 8, 9, and 10. And he's sure that everyone is using every one of those things at every possible moment.

The Disaster Master has learned to beat life at its own game by building up a series of safety nets that can drive you quite mad. Even when things are going great, he's sure that they are about to go bad. For example, on a good day, you may hear him say: "The movers might steal the furniture"; "The electrician will steal your jewelry if you don't hide it"; "The guy in the Chevy is drunk"; "The guy in the Toyota is drunk"; "Temperature changes cause pneumonia"; "TV dinners cause cancer"; "TV causes cancer"; "Cancer causes cancer"; "What if the chicken you just ate had cancer?" (No, he's not brain dead; he just fakes it real well.)

So how do you know if the man you're interested in is a Disaster Master? Let's take it chronologically, or phobialogically. . . .

### Date One

So you have unwittingly met a Disaster Master, and he's asked you for a date. He picks you up at your home and refrains from checking for dust. His nose will tell him where the little buggers are hidden. He sneezes, says, "Damn, I'm coming down with the flu," and looks at you contemptuously. Huh? You get into his midsize Chrysler sedan and, locked up securely in your seat belt, drive to the restaurant. He says he's glad that you didn't have to be coaxed into putting your belt on. Huh?

You arrive at the restaurant where no one knows his name, although everyone knows the *restaurant's* name—Howard Johnson's. (Although it could also be Beefsteak Charlies or, if he's in a spending mood, the local Ramada Inn's Surf & Turf Room.) The only prerequisite? It must have a salad bar. After all, you can load up on salad and take your entrée home for tomorrow's dinner. Now that's value for the dollar!

## What He Won't Do on Dates

- Go to Ethnic or Cozy Places. God only knows what they put in their food, probably puppy.

- Hand Over What He Considers a Whopping Sum of Money for Dinner. (When the next crash comes—and it will, he says—won't those extravagant diners be laughing up their empty sleeves?)

- Use a Utensil Without Wiping It Clean First. If you notice this, and you call him on it, he'll swear he knows of someone who got food poisoning and died from what was caked on his fork in a restaurant.

## Phase Two of Date One

When the waiter comes to bring you menus, D/M says indignantly, "That's okay, we don't need menus, we'll just eat what's left on the tablecloth!" He points to and then brushes off the nonexistent crumbs. The waiter, first embarrassed and then puzzled, offers you another table, where incidentally, another waiter is on duty.

His second brush with death that evening comes while surveying the salad bar. He looks at the dressings and proclaims the whole array the "botulism olympics" and settles for naked lettuce and pickled beets. (Pickled is safe, although God knows they must sneak in MSG and sulfates.) He demands that the lady behind the salad bar who slipped into this country six months ago tell him if there are sulfates and MSG in the pickled beets. She thinks he's a border guard and runs out of the restaurant. He thinks she's suffering from sulfate madness, smiles smugly, and returns the beets with a flourish.

During dinner he will order wine by the glass and ask for bottled water. He holds the glass up to the light to make sure it's clean. He makes no attempt whatsoever to impress you, and although you think he's a bit of a nerd, you can't help but appreciate the fact that he isn't a groper. But be warned: It isn't that he doesn't want to be, it's just that you might be carrying a sexually transmitted disease and he swears he's just heard of someone who died of herpes. You know in your heart that he'd put paper down on the seat of the booth you're sharing, but he's sensitive to criticism, and he's just heard of someone who died from verbal abuse.

## Day In/Day Out

More likely than not, Disaster Master is in one of the less glorified professions. He may be an accountant, an engineer, a technician, the owner of a small electronics retail store. He's not poor, and he's not rich, either. But who knows? He's got everything so tightly secured away in IRA's, AT&T's, and ITB's (in the banks), that no one, including his wife when he marries, ever knows exactly how much he has or doesn't have. But however much it is or isn't, be sure of one thing . . . he doesn't like to share it or shell it out on dates.

After you've known him for a while, you may feel in your heart of hearts that although he's a nice guy, you can't help but imagine what he'd be like if he had a nice comfy electric chair to relax in. You'll fantasize that his Barcalounger turns on him and causes his hair to stand straight up while he himself goes neon. And then of course he has this other problem: the food problem. There are certain foods that he craves and certain foods he fears. Both lists can make you so crazy that you may have to kill him. First . . .

## The Foods He Craves

- Pastina and/or farina
- Cupcakes from scratch with M&M's on the top
- Anything once made by his mother
- Canned soup with crackers broken up in it
- Everything with Hellman's on it
- Everything on his latest diet (it can be all protein one week, complex carbohydrates the next, and whatever the nutritionist said the week after that).

## The Foods He Fears

- Sushi
- Steak that isn't brown
- Eggs (because he heard of a snake hatching from one in a Dairy Barn carton once)
- Mexican food (because he got sick on the water once when he went to Club Med)
- Moo Shu anything

- Food sold from carts, except Good Humor
- Miracle Whip

## The Folks He Loves

- His food allergy doctor who told him he didn't have a brain tumor, but that he *is* allergic to salami
- His cleaning lady
- His pharmacist

## Disaster Master as Boyfriend

Somehow, you end up with him as your boy-friend . . . you just can't help it, he *does* do considerate things that touch you. He will bring your dog to the vet for a checkup, he will watch out for your safety, he will bring your car in for servicing, he will have the drugstore deliver when you have a cold. He locks your doors, and if he deems it necessary, has your locks *changed* (thieves cause cancer); he goes to the grocery store for you, and he straightens up. Unfortunately, he straightens up *his* apartment, right after you do *anything!* A messy apartment (or house, garage, desk, etc.) is a sign of a deranged mind, he reminds you.

He also makes dinner and worries that you'll break a dish and cut yourself if you clean up. While you're cuddled up afterward, he tells you that he's worried. (No kidding.) He thinks his next door neighbor is a hooker and what if her cockroaches carry syphilis? What if a mosquito bit her and then bit him and then he got AIDS? You just stare at him . . . there *is* nothing to say. It's worry without end. *Amen.*

## What He Worries About Before He Marries

- What if I get a chill on my back?

- What would happen if a nuclear attack hit Citibank?

- What if I gain forty pounds by mistake?

- What if they scratch my car in the parking lot?

- What if I park it on the street and they steal my radio?

- What if other people's smoke gave me emphysema?

- What if that small tropical storm turns into a hurricane and hits my house?

- What if I got married and then got divorced, and she took me to the cleaners?

- What if I *stayed* married, and she took me to the cleaners?

- I'm sure I left the iron on.


## What He Worries About After He Marries

- What if I get a chill on my back?

- What if a nuclear attack hits Citibank and only *her* accounts are in First Federal?

- What if she gains forty pounds deliberately?

- What if she shares a car with me and scratches it?

- What if she parks it on the street and they steal my radio?

- What if she starts smoking and gives me emphysema?

- What if that small tropical storm turns into a hurricane and she runs off without first securing the house?

- What if we get divorced, and she takes me to the cleaners?

- What if we don't get divorced, and she takes me to the cleaners?

- What if she had an affair with someone carrying a sexually transmitted disease and didn't admit it until I'd *already* gone blind?

- What if she can't have children?

- What if she wants children and I don't?

- What if she quits her job and refuses to do her share?

- What if we have children and they are drug addicts who smoke cigarettes that give me emphysema? (If *you* already have children from a previous marriage, he's sure that they are drug addicts who smoke cigarettes even if they are preschoolers.)

- I'm sure *she* left the iron on.

## His Background in Brief

Briefly stated, there must have been some schizophrenic pairing of his parents that caused him to become so insecure. But from what you can see, all that his parents are is clean. Now, if D/M was old enough to be drafted when such a thing still existed, you'll be amazed to find out that he wasn't let off for medical reasons. He did in fact serve. Well, he sort of served. Mostly he divided his time between the infirmary and the Chinese laundry near base. Yes, it's true, he sent his sheets out to be done, along with his undies, hat, and uniform.

He also was the only man in the history of the armed forces who enjoyed the V.D. films. He found them moving and informative. But he did grow up a lot during his two-year stint. For example, he learned to drink beer, not write home to mother very often, and buy cameras cheap. Now that's got to account for something!

## What All This Means to You Now: Disaster Master as Mate

"Oh, what a tangled web *you* weave when first *you* practice to deceive," could be his family motto, for quite unexpectedly our mild-mannered D/M becomes a raging bull of jealousy. He's sure you're sleeping with your boss, the dry cleaner, his best friend, your best friend, the dry cleaner's best friend, the postman. He is also sure that you are taking advantage of him by buying Miracle Whip instead of Hellman's and saving the difference (is there even one?) to buy extravagant clothing so that when he dies, you'll have a great wardrobe for your new husband.

It's possible that a lifetime of dirty sex *will* change him. But in case it doesn't, you can always drive him over the brink to normalcy by leaving wet towels on the bed, letting the children leave their roller skates in dangerous places, and by leaving the iron on from time to time, just so that he sees that death is not stalking him, his family, and his friends with every misplaced item.

## What You See and What You Get:
### Disaster Master as Dad

When you are pregnant, he will worry that your unborn will be addicted to Ring Dings, so he hides them from you. He worries that you've picked the wrong doctor, the wrong hospital, and the wrong time to be pregnant. When the baby arrives, he'll want to keep it indoors for the first fifteen years, so it doesn't get sick. He tells you all babysitters are perverts and morons, and so are all kids in schools.

He therefore teaches his children the dangers of strangers, including members of your family (not his). Consequently, when other kids are rebelling by getting into drugs, sex, and rock and roll, your children rebel by sneaking off to Burger King for Whoppers with everything, including the secret sauce that everyone knows is Miracle Whip. When they come of age, they drag him to a taco stand, where he nearly faints.

Luckily your children will be more you than him, and if he learns to lighten up and stop worrying that they will fall out of a tree, in front of a car, and off their bikes, he'll be a most caring—if neurotic—papa. But chances are good that poor D/M will never survive *your* labor pains. If he does manage to live through them, extreme caution is advised, especially if you allow him into the delivery room with you. Even though he loves the experience, he may never be able to forgive you for making such a mess.

**BEST OF BREED**

**Disaster Master**

Most Likely to Keep Running:
RALPH NADER

Seems Like It but Obviously Isn't:
WOODY ALLEN

Most Blatant in Literature:
GARP

Must Be in the Closet:
JOHN IRVING

The One with No Shame Whatsoever:
NOSTRADAMUS

## IMPOSSIBLE MAN #4

# Born to Bank

Every woman who has ever lived in a large city has met and/or mated at least one Born to Bank in her time. You know who he is because, like the American Express card that he carries, he is internationally recognized—or at least recognizable. Why? Because he looks like his brothers in arms the world over. He dresses, acts, and says the same things whether he is a certified eastern yuppie, a southern good old boy, or a middle-eastern heir to the chair. (That can be loosely translated as throne, bank, or gusher, if you like.)

You may first spot him at a party that is

given by the captain of his college's girls' field hockey team; she is very rich and has thick calves. The "food" at her party consists of a lot of booze and one bowl of tortilla chips. There may be one or two really frightening hors d'oeuvres as well. The hostess of this do shares her one-bedroom apartment with a roommate who looks like her twin. They give many of these parties because they miss college mixers, and because they are becoming insane now that everyone that they know is getting married (with one exception each).

## His Clothes Encounters

Born to Bank loves his party clothes, and you know that you're in the right place if all the "girls" are dressed up and all the "boys" are dressed down. He is wearing: Gucci loafers without socks (if the temperature is anywhere above 36 degrees); if it is colder than 36 degrees, he will wear yellow or some other equally inappropriate color. He thinks it's wild; everyone else thinks it's tasteless. He will be wearing khakis if it's summer, and khakis if it's winter. But if he comes straight from work, you can expect to find him in a Paul Stuart or (increasingly, as they get older) a custom-made suit.

In the winter he wears chalk stripe or blue or gray solid. In summer, it's light colors, and after hours, gray seersucker from J. Press. He sports a stainless-steel Rolex, silk-knot cuff links from Paul Stuart or monogrammed gold ones. If he's not wearing a Rolex, he's wearing a beat-up old Timex-looking something with a ribbon band that he changes often and well. He may also have taken recently to wearing suspenders, but he calls them "braces." He has never worn, nor

43

does he ever intend to wear, an undershirt (not even as an infant). But no one (except his buddies in the locker room and his girlfriends), ever knows this, because he has never left even one button open on a shirt in his life (not even as an infant). That, in his opinion, would be going Hollywood . . . or worse . . . going garment-o.

He wears his hair relatively short, but if he thinks of himself as a little funky (that is, he goes to the newest underground clubs the second they open and may open one himself soon), he might wear his hair very short on the sides and very long on the top. When he stands near an open window, you realize that he looks identical to the crazed star of *Reefer Madness* before he took the fatal leap. This, however, is *not* considered going Hollywood.

Remember, though, if the party is held anywhere other than this girl's apartment, it will definitely be black tie and he will definitely *not* have to visit the "After-Six" shop to rent a tux before the party.

### Phase One: Party Talk

Born to Banks come in two party varieties, the banal and the outrageous, or in other words the extraordinarily rich and the just plain rich. It does not mean that the outrageous talker is not loaded . . . he's just not *as* loaded. For our purposes we'll start with:

### Approach One: Seriously Banal
### [His Way]

HE SAYS:   So, how do you know Lisa?

HE MEANS: Has Lisa told you how good I am in bed?

HE SAYS: So, what do you do? Where do you work?

HE MEANS: Wait till she hears that I'm in the fast-paced glamorous world of high finance.

HE SAYS: Where do you live?

HE MEANS: I wonder how she stacks up . . . financially?

HE SAYS: Really? How much do they [did they] get you for? (Depending on whether you bought or rent . . .)

HE MEANS: Is she getting a better deal on her apartment than I'm getting on mine? I wonder if her family owns the building, I wonder what space is left?

HE SAYS: So, where did you go to school?

HE MEANS: I went to Harvard, or . . .

Somewhere in the conversation, you exchange cards. The last you see of him is when one of you goes to get a drink. However, much to your surprise, he calls you a few days later and asks you out.

### Approach Two: Outrageous
### [His Way]

He comes up to you in the middle of the party, after he's not noticed you to your knowledge (although you've noticed him, God knows), and . . .

HE SAYS: So, do you want to go out or what?

SHE SAYS: I beg your pardon?

HE SAYS: I said, do you want to go out or what?

SHE SAYS: Excuse me, but I don't even know who you are.

HE SAYS: Do you like jazz?

SHE SAYS: But what's your name?

HE SAYS: Gerry Mulligan.

SHE SAYS: That's it, I'm not talking to you anymore.

HE SAYS: Okay, okay, it's Richard . . . Mulligan.

SHE SAYS: It's nice to meet you. I'm Sarah . . . Vaughn.

HE SAYS: [laughing] Here's my card. Call me and we'll go hear jazz.

SHE SAYS: A: I don't call men I don't know, and B: I don't call men and ask them out.

HE SAYS: No? Then why are we having this conversation?

SHE SAYS: Hey wait a minute! You brought the whole thing up.

HE SAYS: I did? Okay, then give me your card.

SHE SAYS: (Haughtily) I don't have a card.

HE SAYS: (As he hands her a napkin) Write.

Somehow, you find that you're writing your number down and handing it to someone who might, for all you know, be a mass murderer. You don't see him again the whole evening, and then you notice he's gone. But not forgotten. He calls within the next two weeks.

## Both Conversations:
## Your Way
### (After the first few words are exchanged)

SHE SAYS: Here's my card . . . and [looking around] there's my date.

If you were foolish enough to show up at this party without one, substitute any male friend and grab his arm. (You can give him the scoop later.)

### Date One: Drugs, Sex, and Rest-au-rants

You meet him at a restaurant that is known for its preppiness. It is upper-middle range, which makes you slightly uncomfortable when the bill comes. He would never never expect you to pay . . . but he *does* expect you to offer, so that he can look aghast at your suggestion.

You will learn during the evening that he is probably promiscuous, but that he is promiscuous in the same way that he drinks too much beer. Both are a rite of passage that he will discontinue the second he settles down. You will also learn that his briefcase contains: king-size bottles of aspirin, Pepto-Bismol, and Afrin. Aspirin is the drug of choice for his high-pressure arbitrage deals, Pepto-Bismol is the drug of choice the morning after the night before when he acted like he was still living in a dorm, and Afrin is the drug of choice the morning after the night before, so that he can get his nose working again.

One more word about his indiscriminate sex: He is the only promiscuous man in the world who has indiscriminate sex with women he's known since he was five. (He may be indiscriminate, but he's not careless!) His father had to be

47

careless from time to time because this was before the pill and not everyone in his crowd did
"it." He's been heard more than once to thank
God for Johnson & Johnson and coed dorms.

## What's Hot

Born to Bank is into everything that is chic and
glamorous, and he knows the latest hot everything. By the time that Trivial Pursuit began to
appear on the store shelves, for example, he'd
long given it up and was already becoming
bored with Scruples (the game). He also became
bored with vodka and traded it for single malt
Scotch and tapas. He loves Bermuda, frequent-
flyer programs, talking stocks, and visiting his
parents' country house.

## What's Cold

If you begin to wonder what he'd be like in bed,
take him dancing. He dances the same way that
he makes love. If he's a smooth dancer, chances
are good he's a smooth lover. If he dips and
swirls and makes a complete show of himself,
he's more interested in *his* technique than in
*your* pleasure. Finally, beware the manic
lindy/twister. In bed, it's a brief but frenzied
motion that suddenly stops. He will immediately
take a shower, leaving you saying to yourself,
"Excuse me a minute, what was *that* all about?
Or better yet, what *was* that?"

Beware, too, the Born to Bank who creates
an ear ocean with fancy tongue action that can
leave you with a serious case of swimmer's ear
after one good old-fashioned make-out session.

And what does *he* like in bed himself? Well,
it's well known that he likes oral sex. A lot. Especially when he's on the receiving end, no pun

intended. He *is* after all in a service industry, and he doesn't separate what he does for a living from what he does for fun.

## Your Wicked, Wicked Past

Surprise! He's jealous! And he's jealous of every man you've ever known, particularly your former boyfriends. He will fear that you were a sex slave who was always begging for "it." Tell him that you never knew what it was all about until you did it with him. He won't believe you, but it may temporarily stop him from obsessing about your status as sex-slave. Since he doesn't like to date outside the periphery of his own crowd, chances are good that you have dated all of his friends at some point and he will quiz you constantly about how they stack up next to him. Lie.

## Your Not Uncertain Future

Understand right off the bat that this man was programmed to be married for the first time between twenty-seven and thirty-four. His father did it at that age, as did his father before him, and so will he. He expects to be married, he wants to be married, and if he's chosen you to marry, he expects you to go along with it.

He will settle down immediately after getting married, and expects his wife to become physically attached to a station wagon. He expects to have blond, blue-eyed children, even if he's of a different race, and he expects them to be able to roughhouse with the best of them at a moment's notice. Therefore . . .

. . . if Born to Bank's son ever told him that he wanted to:

1. Take ballet lessons
2. Go to a camp for creative children
3. Take singing lessons

he'd suspect that you'd been sleeping around nine months prior to the birth of this child. And he'd be right. Even if you are an actress, singer, ballet dancer, or artist yourself, your son simply will not be. It's in the genes—his.

Your daughters, on the other hand (yes, there will be many children), will be a perfect melding of the two of you. These are the girls who grow up to be Ford models who win Nobel Prizes and have great legs.

Therefore, you must really like this man before you have children with him, or you'll be stuck with perfect children who call themselves Biff, Chip, and Bootsy.

Born to Bank will make a good, if not exciting, husband. (His obsession with too much sex is transferred immediately upon signing the marriage certificate into sports, investments, Little League, etc., etc., etc.) He has lots of money, and he likes beautiful homes, children, and clothing. In other words, he's very social. You'll never be bored outside of the bedroom, but unless you can teach him a few less-than-social graces, you could end up with swimmer's ear . . . a predictable three times a week. For life.

## BEST OF BREED

### Born to Bank

Best Role Model:
GEORGE PLIMPTON

Funny . . . He Sure Doesn't
Look Bankish:
IVAN BOESKY

Funny . . . He Sure *Does*
Look Bankish:
WILLIAM BUCKLEY

Best of Brood:
Anyone Named
KENNEDY
Who Was Born After 1958

Close But No Cigar:
PRINCE ANDREW*

Best Performance by an Actor
Who Missed His Calling:
GEORGE HAMILTON

*Due to circumstances beyond his control, Randy Andy is not allowed to be a multinational bank-type, since his family already owns England. He was allowed to play army, but he quit because they wouldn't let him wear his crown in the cockpit.

**IMPOSSIBLE MAN #5**

## No Shame/No Gain

**B**eware the man with no shame who is proud of the fact that he speaks like a Hallmark card. He is the man you'll meet while recovering from the breakup of a true affair of the heart. That's the only time you'd be insane enough to think he's sweet and sensitive. But even if you're a Noble Peace Prize winner who's walking around with stigmata, you'll eventually complain that you can never get a good gangland style rub-out when you need one.

But since he'll find you when you are at your most vulnerable, you'll go around for about fifteen minutes, saying things to your friends like,

"Gee, what a sweet guy." *Then* he begins to give you tooth decay.

You'll recognize a No Shame right off the bat because after one date he assumes you have a relationship, and nothing can dissuade him from his own truth. Does he behave this way because he can't ever get a woman interested in him? Hardly. In fact, lots of women are after him, because he is, after all, a very attractive man. The problem isn't the women who want him, it's . . .

### The Women He Wants

Shameless tends to go for women who are in unusual, even isolating professions. So, if you are a writer, painter, designer, or are in any other profession that keeps you alone a lot, beware. It's not that he's a murdering pervert; he's just boring—and women with lots of co-workers don't need to talk to a living Hallmark card at eleven in the morning. But even a cloistered nun would yell obscenities into the phone to this one after he wished her a day of sunshine and rainbows.

### The No-Shame Mating Game

Here's how you can tell right away if you are about to become ensnared in the Shameless web. You might be introduced to him at a party, he might be the guy who gets the toilet paper for you on the high shelf in the supermarket, you might spill coffee on him at a local football game . . . in other words, no place is safe.

He will ask you for your number on the spot, and then you'll have to wait for him to call, which intrigues you. That's the last intriguing thing he'll ever do. On your first date, he'll give you the story of his life, which is not nearly as tragic as he'd hoped for. Even so, he manages to look upset as he stares off into space every few paragraphs. Right then, you've got to know that this guy's not for real. He'll squint his eyes at you in an inane attempt to be sexy and mean-ingful all at once.

He mistakes the fact that your body is going into hypoglycemic shock for love, and he smiles knowingly. Strangely enough, he also manages at the same time to flirt with every woman in the place. This unfortunately has nothing to do with what you can only hope is his waning inter-est in you. It's then that he says his first truly embarrassing thing (while he's lighting another woman's cigarette, yet!). . . .

HE SAYS: I can tell that you're feeling the same things I'm feeling.

HE MEANS: They just can't get enough of me.

SHE SAYS: I beg your pardon?

SHE MEANS: What an asshole.

HE SAYS: This might seem crazy, but you make me want to do things like go fly a kite.

HE MEANS: They love it when I talk like that.

SHE SAYS: I don't feel well.

SHE MEANS: What an asshole.

HE SAYS: Oooo, the pooooor babeeee.

HE MEANS: I guess *she's* not gonna get lucky tonight.

SHE SAYS: I've got to go.

SHE MEANS: Let me out of here!

HE SAYS: I'll take you home.

HE MEANS:  I knew it . . . she wants me to take her to bed.

SHE SAYS:  No! Really! The subway is just fifty-three blocks from here!

You dash out of there and run for your life into the subway. An attempted mugging on the platform makes you feel better. Anything beats listening to him recite from the Andy Williams school of soul.

You think you've gotten rid of him, but he'll continue to leave messages on your answering machine that *sound* like smile faces *look*. When he does get you on the phone, he speaks in insane double entendres that make you want to scream. If you say that you can't talk because you are dripping wet from the shower, he'll ask you if you need someone to come wipe you down. If you say it's snowing he'll ask you how many inches . . . heh, heh, heh. Everything is an excuse for him to say something horrifying. He thinks you love this talk, because he also thinks, for some bizarre reason, that he is your boyfriend.

### His Heartbreaking Background

How does someone *get* like this? Obviously it has something to do with child abuse. He was most likely chained to a TV set and forced to watch every special ever created by the Osmonds, *and* the King family. There's a good chance that his parents met while on tour with "Up with People," as a matter of fact.

He talks often and well about his parents. He loves them. And he also probably has another group of people he calls his family. Yes, it's true: he, a grown man, still calls the family that owned the house he boarded in for one semester his parents! (They might also be the parents of his best friend when he was growing up.)

## The Great Escape

So how do you escape? You've stood him up, you've told him that you hate him, you've insulted him, laughed in his face, refused his calls, ignored him at parties, and still he calls and shamelessly leaves messages on your machine like, "How'd you like to get naked and jump into a hot tub with me?" You are beyond being embarrassed for his lack of shame, insight, judgment, taste, sanity, and depth.

Unfortunately the only way to get rid of him is to break up with him. Huh? How can you break up with someone you've only dated once or twice? Look, you know you're not involved, but he doesn't. It doesn't make sense, but then again, neither does he . . . so when in Rome . . .

Tell him that although it will be tough on you you've got to devote yourself full time to your career, your dying grandmother, your orthodontic work, your kyaking, your pot weaving, your whatever. If you don't think he'll swallow this, go for the big one and pray that that you get away with it.

## The Breakup: Your Way

SHE SAYS:      I have to break up because you've hurt me too much.

SHE THINKS:    Please, God, I'll go to church every day for the rest of my life if this works.

HE SAYS:       I didn't mean to. I'm sorry.

SHE SAYS:      That's the whole point. You never mean to, but you always do.

| | |
|---|---|
| SHE THINKS: | I hope this doesn't take much longer, the Channel Five Movie Club is on in an hour. |
| HE SAYS: | I swear I'll never do it again. (Huh?) |
| SHE SAYS: | I'm sorry. I just can't continue this. |
| HE SAYS: | I want to stay friends with you, because I understand where you're coming from. |

If you can deal with this deal, it's not a bad one. He will, after all, do things like help you to move, put up shelves, and take you to the movies when no one's around.

## The Best Defense

Now, how do you stop all of this before it even begins? The best defense is of course a good offense. Therefore, learn to spot him on sight. If you are in doubt, check out his appearance.

**He Wears:** Not-terribly-well-cut clothing, and an expensive haircut. Yes, he visits the same hairdresser you do.

**He Wants:** to sail or fly into the forever, the sunset, never-never land, around the world to where the sea and sky are one. The man is truly without shame.

**He Does:** write embarrassing poetry, buy you a balloon, love children, dogs, and women who don't seem to care whether he lives or drowns in his own hot tub.

**He Sends:** Ziggy cards, dumb dirty cards, and poetry books that he actually buys in card shops.

**He Also:** Drives a Honda, drinks vodka, and may own his own house. He has attended public school, and his mother looks like Betty White and his father looks like Caesar Romero. His folks still play bridge with the neighbors, and his mother still makes her husband's shirts, complete with monogram. He wants a girl just like the girl, and thank God they don't make them like that anymore.

## BEST OF BREED

### No Shame/No Gain

Most Embarrassing Display of
No Shame in Publishing:
**ROD McKUEN**

All Around Shameless:
**BARRY MANILOW**

The Most Shameless Shrink:
**LEO BUSCAGLIA**

Ad Nauseum: East of the Rockies:
**JOHN DAVIDSON**

Ad Nauseum: West of the Rockies:
**JOHN DENVER**

Shameless Hall of Fame:
**ROBERT GOULET**

**WAYNE NEWTON**

No Shame Hall of Fame:
Entire Families Without Shame:
**THE KING FAMILY
INCLUDING ALBINO REY**

**THE PARTRIDGE FAMILY**

**THE BRADY BUNCH**

**IMPOSSIBLE MAN #6**

# Hit and Missing

---

### The Man Who Refuses/Forgets/Can't Bring Himself to Call Back Until:
*(CHECK ONE)* ☐ Months later ☐ Never

---

**W**ithout this man, there would be no such thing as institutions for mental health. And even though he should be confined to one forever, he escapes his fate by simply being content to be the subject of endless talk to endless shrinks by endless women who've been run down by him. He is simply the best of breed (when it comes to Impossible Men, anyway), and he never wavers . . . and he doesn't—repeat doesn't—change for anyone. He can make you insane, and he'll never know it because he doesn't call back after the best date you've ever had in your whole life.

"Why would someone *do* that?" you screech to your mother, your best friend, your shrink, your other boyfriends, even. But nobody's talking. Of course, they'll say things like, "He knows you're too good for him, that's why"; "He'd never belong to any club that would have him for a member, that's why"; "Maybe he's married"; "Maybe he's attracted to you too strongly"; "Maybe he's afraid of getting tied down"; "Maybe he'll call back"; "Maybe he's had to take a business trip"; "Maybe he's gay"; "Maybe he's sick in bed"; "Maybe he's dead"; or maybe he's just nuts, which is the closest to the truth you're ever going to get. He *is* crazy, and *he* doesn't even know why he doesn't call back.

Maybe he thinks he shouldn't, or maybe he never seems to get any fallout from it. But you assume this man simply wouldn't have survived this long behaving this way to every woman he dated . . . would he? Yes.

He *knows* how difficult it is to say to someone whom you've only been out with once or twice, "Gee, where have you been? I thought we had a good thing going." And that's especially hard when you just *know* that he'll look at you as if you've lost your mind.

Unfortunately, however, if one of these guys has ever hit and run out of your life, you simply will never forget him, although you can't for the life of you figure out why. Maybe it was that he was utterly charming, or maybe he made you feel utterly charming yourself. How can you tell if you're about to get almost involved with a Hit and Missing man? Study carefully the . . .

## Hit and Missing M.O.

When Hit and Missing meets a woman, you can be sure that he seems like a dream package.

He's fun—charming, witty, sexy, and he seems so *there*. He takes your number, he calls within two weeks, and he sounds as adorable on the phone as you remembered him to be in person. Let's take a look at . . .

## Conversation Numero Uno: His Way

HE SAYS: Hi! This is Jim. I met you at the party the other night?

HE MEANS: Hi. This is Jim, the one you've been sitting by the phone waiting for for two weeks now.

SHE SAYS: Party? Oh, yes, I remember.

SHE MEANS: I was giving it two more hours. If you didn't call by then, I was attaching myself to an extension cord and taking a bath.

HE SAYS: Gee, I'd like to get together and get to know you.

HE MEANS: I'm overextended on my American Express, I'm busy for the next three weeks, I need to get laid, and if you've any decency at all, you'll sense my urgency and offer to cook.

SHE SAYS: Well, let me check my appointment book before I commit to anything.

SHE MEANS: The last appointment in this book was lunch with Mamie Eisenhower . . . maybe I can lose twenty-six pounds by tomorrow night.

SHE SAYS: Gee, umm, let's see. I think I can move things around. How's tomorrow or Tuesday the fifth look for you?

SHE MEANS: How's Tuesday the fifth through Wednesday the thirty-first and possibly the rest of your life?

HE SAYS: Gee, I was thinking more like a week from next Thursday.

HE MEANS: She's chomping at the bit. How much did I drink anyway? Is this the one that looks like Marvin Hamlish?

## Conversation Numero Uno: Your Way

HE SAYS: Hi. This is Jim. I met you at the party the other night?

SHE SAYS: Party?

HE SAYS: The party that Kevin gave?

SHE SAYS: Oh.

HE SAYS: I'd like to get together and get to know you.

SHE SAYS: How about three weeks from next Thursday?

## Phase Two

Don't be upset. Know that he won't call you again until the afternoon of your date . . . which is three hundred years away. You will think he has forgotten. You should only be that lucky.

## Phase Three

He will meet you in a restaurant. You arrive late, looking divine. Of course you have walked around the block forty-three times in a desperate attempt to appear not desperate by (please, God!) arriving after he does. Step one: It seems to have worked. He's already at the bar. Step two: It hasn't. He's used this time creatively. He's now on a first-name basis with the "I'm-really-an-actress-and-model-but-I'm-working-here-to-help-me-get-through-law-school" bartender. She has no thighs. Through the miracle of high-speed water retention, your thighs, on the other hand, are quickly beginning to resemble something better saved as a flying companion to Bullwinkle at the Thanksgiving Day parade. Speedy ascension to the table is required at this time. You hope the waiters don't keep time to your thighs as you make your way across the room. You lie and say you're wearing taffeta pantyhose. In the meantime, "thighless" passes you carrying a tray that yanks her adorable denim miniskirt even higher, which even a moment ago seemed impossible. You pray that she becomes the tragic victim of cellulite, but the chances of that happening are as slim as she is.

He orders wine when she comes to the table. At least you know that he knows that she's not your intellectual equal. Then she jokes around with him . . . in Latin. You are now beside yourself. Then he speaks to *you*.

HE SAYS: I was hoping I remembered correctly and I did. You really *are* pretty.

HE MEANS: You *really* are pretty.

SHE SAYS: Thanks. So are you.

SHE MEANS: I'm going to faint.

HE SAYS: Have you decided what you want?

HE MEANS: Just what he said.

SHE SAYS: No, not really.

SHE MEANS: Yes, and he's sitting opposite me.

The dinner arrives, and he eats heartily, joking around and never, ever saying anything like "You're pretty" again. You, on the other hand, can't bear to touch one morsel, and push your food around like a three-year-old and try to get him to say "You're pretty" or any other such nicety again. You resort finally to things like:

"Gee, this is fun. I enjoy being with you"; "I'm glad you called . . . I had forgotten that I met you"; "We should try this [that, or anything] sometime." From none of these hints do you get a response. You give up and feel more petulant than you admit to. He senses it and comes around a little bit. Dinner is over and he hasn't said one thing (!) about seeing you again. What (in reality) should you do? How about just trying to have a nice time without worrying about how you're doing!

## What Happens Next

You leave the restaurant, and now the real trauma begins. Does he expect to take you home and hop into bed? The nerve! Or will he not even make an attempt? The nerve! Well, since there are two possible ends to your first date, there are two possible scenarios.

## Scenario #1

You get into a cab and . . .

HE SAYS:     What's your address?

HE MEANS:   What's your address?

SHE SAYS:     1407 Bayview Avenue.

SHE MEANS:  Is he dropping me off, or is he coming upstairs? Do I invite him up, or is that a come on? Why do I do this

> to myself? I wish I were home right
> now watching reruns of "The Hon-
> eymooners" in my bathrobe. Alone.
> Without ever having met this guy.

You ride in silence, partly because you are so
tense that you are beginning to resemble an em-
ery board, partly because he doesn't see the
need to make any conversation at this point.
You are going slightly mad. Is he going to reject
you, or are you going to reject him and then
never see him again? Of course, you consciously
know that in real life you've rejected hundreds
of men's first-date attempts, and it has never
stopped them from calling back. Even so . . .

The moment of truth: The driver stops at
your house. Is he coming up or not? He pays
the driver and gets out of the cab *with* you. It's
too late, you *are* hyperventilating. Oh, my God!
Does he think that your heavy breathing comes
from uncontrolled passion? You get to your
door.

HE SAYS: Nothing.

HE MEANS: Should I spend the night, or should
I go home afterward because I have
to get that case prepared for the
morning?

SHE SAYS: Would you like to come in for a
drink or something?

SHE MEANS: Why did I say that?

HE SAYS: Of course. (Surprised)

HE MEANS: No, of course not. I make a living by
standing outside of people's doors
after I let the ride go.

SHE SAYS: (or blurts out) Good. But I'm not
going to sleep with you.

SHE MEANS: Huh?

HE SAYS: So who asked you?

SHE SAYS: You will.

HE SAYS: You're right!

Now the tension is broken and everyone feels a lot better. Somehow or other, he's showering in your bathroom the next morning. Damn!

## Scenario #2

He hails a cab. It stops, and he opens the door for you. You are nervously wondering if he will drop you off or attempt to come in when you get home. After you get into the cab, he closes the door, sticks his head in through the window, and gives you a little kiss. Then you are somehow driving off into the night sans date . . . and sanity.

You go home enraged. How could he do this to you? Does he hate you? Does he like you? He gave no indication of either. You are really angry, sort of. The days pass, and you are beginning to moon over him. He doesn't call and you are miserable. Why? You didn't even have that good a time, you tell your friends. Out of the blue (months later), he calls at a totally inappropriate time, like seven o'clock on Saturday night. You talk for fifteen minutes, and he doesn't ask you out. One minute before he hangs up he says something truly maddening like, "Well, we should have lunch sometime." Lunch? Yes, lunch. You say something like, "Gee, lunch is bad for me because I never seem to get out of my office. Dinner is better." He says that's okay, and makes a date for three weeks away. Again. You have dinner, you go through the same frightening out of control evening, and somehow he is showering in your bathroom the next morning. Damn!

## Getting Paroled

Now, the truth of it is, the scenarios are different but the ending isn't. It doesn't seem to end, in fact. If you allow it, it can be a lifelong *almost* relationship.

He doesn't call you the morning after, and in fact, he doesn't usually call at all for months. You are furious with yourself for sleeping with a man whom you are too embarrassed to call. How could you have done all of those embarrassing things (with your clothes off, for God's sake!) with someone you don't have the nerve to call? You moan and whine to everyone who will listen for the next two months, and he slowly begins to recede from your mind.

Six months later he calls as though he is simply an old friend who's checking in and it starts all over again.

Unfortunately this can go on for the rest of your life, because there's something magical about him . . . although for the life of you, you can't figure out what it is.

## Real Life Scenario #3

Let's face it, it's really tough to play hard to get with someone who only shows up every six months. I mean, really, what can you do, tell him that you've been unavailable for the last six months? How about simply saying (*before* he does), "Well, I've got to run, but let's have lunch someday. I'll call you." Then don't. After all, this is not a relationship . . . *this* is a sentence.

## BEST OF BREED

### Hit and Missing

From the What-Do-You-Feed-
A-Five-Hundred-Pound-Gorilla-
School-
of-Give-Him-Anything-He-Wants:

WARREN BEATTY

The Evelyn Woods Driving School
Award:

TED KENNEDY

Most Often Dated With
the Most Dated Hairdo:

ROD STEWART

Honorable Mention for Serial
Monogamy:

JOHNNY CARSON

**IMPOSSIBLE MAN #7**

## Mama-Son

**B**eware the man who loves his mother's macaroni and cheese more than he loves sex. Or you. Or anything. This is the classic sign of a Mama's fave. It's not that he doesn't love women. After all, his mother is one. It's just that he learned early on that loving one (a woman, *any* woman) more than, or even as much as, his mother, could and probably *would* kill her (his mother, that is).

Now although this relationship (his with *her* versus his with *you*) leads you to imagine (especially if this is your first one) that he and his mother trade clothes and set each other's hair, it's simply not so. That's not to say that they haven't spent many a misty Saturday antiquing and hitting the swap meets for vintage wicker and God-knows-what-else together. But he's really never worn her clothes. Except for laughs.

I can hear you, even now, saying to yourself, "Ho, ho, ha, ha, not me. I would be able to spot a loser like that from a mile away!" Hmmm. Yes? Maybe. But probably not. Mama's favorite son doesn't necessarily go around garbed in sheep's clothing, you know. In fact, he's probably spent a good deal of time garbed in wolf's clothing . . . or what he considers wolf's clothing. Unfortunately he still uses the term "wolf" to mean a "svinger," so his clothing is usually an embarrassingly bad attempt at hipness, worldliness, or style.

Alas, he lacks hipness, worldliness, and style, thanks to the woman who gave him life. If you doubt my word, test him. Chances are good that: 1) He's been to at least one Wayne Newton or Barry Manilow show in Las Vegas or Atlantic City; 2) he's not ashamed to admit that the farthest he's been from his home town (of his own free will besides the company trip to Las Vegas or Atlantic City) was to Club Med, where he nearly lost his mind at the sight of so much flesh; and 3) he still owns (and has been seen wearing) a Huckapoo shirt and/or gold chain. The other possibilities get downright frightening, and there's no sense getting ugly early on.

## How You Meet

It's not hard to meet Mr. Mom. He does, after all, hold down a job, and he does go to singles' things. Usually he holds a job in some kind of civil service organization, where he may be a supervisor of something ambiguous like systems-testing production or a special-procedures evaluation unit. No one, except Mr. Mom and Mom herself, knows exactly what it is that he does. But chances are good that he's been told that he does it real well. Chances are even better that no one except he and Mom are even sure that he goes to work every day. In fact, if you asked one of his fellow workers whether he was at work yesterday, they'd have to think a couple minutes before answering.

At any rate, you might meet him at the company Christmas party (he doesn't bring his mother), or the company picnic (where he may be forced to drink too much beer because he feels guilty that he didn't bring his mother *and* didn't even visit her before he left, even though it was a Sunday). If it is the Christmas party, you somehow end up dancing one dance with him, which he does well, if a bit stiffly. If it's the company picnic, you notice that he pitches the curve ball in the softball game your way once too often. He blushes when you call him on it after the game. He blushes when you flirt with him, even though he's already feeling very little pain.

Sweet, you think. Nice, you think. A decent guy for a change, you think. So, okay, he *is* a bit of a nerd, and he does get himself done up at times like a mad cross between Sonny Bono and Mr. Rogers, you can always teach him to dress. You think. What you are not aware of at the time is that he gives a whole new dimension to the phrase, "You're ugly, and your mother dresses you funny."

## What He Does on Your First Date

• Talk about his mother.

• Talk about his mother's neighbors. (They

don't appreciate the effort she makes to keep the neighborhood decent!)

- Talk about how his brother(s) and/or sister(s) moved out of town and didn't offer to move back when his father died and/or retired, and life became tough on Mom.

- Take you to the movies and to a diner for hamburgers afterward.

- Drive you home and walk you to your door not expecting to come in unless you live at home with your parents, and then he would love to come in and have coffee with your mother.

### What He Does on Your Second Date

- Try to get lucky.

### What He Does on Your Third Date

- Take you to his cousin's wedding.

### What He Does on Your Fourth Date

- Cancel. His mother called him at work to say she's had a fainting spell.

### What He Does on Your Fifth Date

- Get stood up, if you're smart. No sense in trying to compete with you-know-who. The most you can hope for if you continue is that he'll marry you just when she gets around to needing a full-time nurse!

Remember, in the mama's boy category it's better if he has a live wife than a mother who's still breathing. Worried that he's married? Who cares? The only prerequisite should be dead parents.

Okay, so you think, "I've gone too far." Ha! You will be saying the same thing every Sunday of your life when Mom is making her famous chicken and rice just for you (him).

Here's how it goes: She invites you early in your relationship to her house for dinner. She fusses over you and smooths the fabric of your dress as she smiles warmly. What a sweet thing, she says about you. What a dear woman, you say about her. Then you make the mistake of going to the bathroom, and she stabs you in the back. Women of your religion sleep with various farm animals, she's heard. Women of your nationality drink. She knows that for a fact. And dirty? Wow! Did he ever remember visiting Joey's mother's house growing up? Not that she let him go there but once . . . but even once was enough. Laundry piled up for a week at least, and the woman didn't know what an iron was, for God's sake! If he's willing to take on that kind of life . . . well, he can be her guest, but she hopes she doesn't live long enough to see it. Somehow, he's different when you come back into the room.

Now, don't get me wrong; Mama-Son is a nice, if not especially exciting guy. And his mother seems sweet, if a bit whiny. He's usually the last- or first-born son, and he honestly feels in his heart of hearts that his mother couldn't manage without him. He believes that he does everything for her, even if he doesn't.

If you feel you must have him to call your own, then you must be everything his mother has warned him about. Be a crazed nymphomanical stripping vampire who insists on taking him to nude beaches where you feed him cold chicken while he's lying on his back. Send him erotic chocolates at work without a card, teach him to smoke pot in your living room, buy him an oversized rag sweater from L. L. Bean, and take him trout fishing and then take him white-water rafting on the Colorado River. (He pays, of course.) When he calls you from his mother's house, be completely tasteless and tell him that you're hungry and have no one to eat. When he asks you, tell him you're crazy about his mother but don't go with him when he visits, no matter how much you hate her.

Then find a new boyfriend to occupy your time when he's with Mom. Even he will crumble under this onslaught, even she will capitulate. He will hire someone to cut her grass (when he knows he should be doing it), to be with you . . . and to make sure you are not being a stripping vampire who is white-water rafting with someone else.

## Mama's Favorite Son, Moon, and Stars as Mate

Somehow through the miracle of high-speed sleight of hand, you do get wonder-son to marry you. What kind of husband and father will he make? Not as good at either as he is at being a son, that's for sure. His mother's illnesses will always come before his wife's or his kids'. His mother will continue to fuss over him when he comes in the door, and to give you an air kiss. She will like the children because they are his, but she will never love them because they are also yours. You will find yourself bundling up children with colds and sore throats for Sunday visits to Nana's. You will get sick and tired of her constant, "Really, it's nothing, just a little heart attack/cancer/stroke . . . don't ruin your plans just to come over and get me an ambulance/doctor/off the floor and back into my iron lung."

She'll invite you to her garage sale where everything you've ever given her is on sale. You'll ask for the unused wok back, and she'll say, "Sure. That'll be $10.50."

But my dear, my dear, what will you have won if you win? A lifetime subscription to *Prevention*, and the constant chore of finding new and different exotic undies to lure him back home? Is that really what you want . . . no matter how crazy not being able to have him all to yourself can make any normally secure woman? And besides, what if you finally *do* turn him normal? Then you just know he'll resent *you* for it when she kicks the bucket. That's when he'll decide that he needs to find someone more understanding. Someone more like his mother.

**BEST OF BREED**

**Mama-son**

Aren't You Being a Little Extreme
in Terms of Your Mother? Award:

NORMAN BATES

Weren't You Being a Little Extreme
in Terms of Your Mother
and Her Clothing? Award:

LIBERACE

Aren't You Being a Little Extreme
in Terms of Your Mother Who
Needed a Mobile Home So She Could
Follow You Around When You Got
Drafted? Award:

ELVIS PRESLEY

**IMPOSSIBLE MAN #8**

# Dan, Dan the Married Man

**W**hat can you say about Dan besides the fact that he's married? Well, you can say that he fools around. He says he doesn't (except in this particular case, with you, if you happen to be the girlfriend on the side), but he does. Well, he does, unless of course you're married to him and then he probably doesn't fool around. With you. What he does do with or *to* you (if you're his wife), is make occasional love . . . which is different from fooling around—occasionally or habitually.

If Dan isn't *your* husband, then you've probably met him at or through your job, and he may or may not admit his connubial arrangement to you right off the bat. One type lies and pretends to be divorced while the other type feels compelled to tell you within the first five minutes of meeting you that: 1) he's married; 2) he never cheats on his wife; and 3) he and his wife don't sleep together. At this point you can say, "Excuse me, but who asked?" and then you can tell him that you've recently discovered that only 50 percent of all married people sleep together. It seems that all the wives sleep with their husbands, but none of the husbands sleep with their wives. If that doesn't shut him up, you're probably in trouble.

## What He Was Like Then . . .
## What He's Like Now

Unlike his 1950s counterpart, the modern Dan is a hip, unsleazy guy. (So it seems.) If, however, he is over the age of fifty, he will wear suits that have been tailored too much and he may even have a hairdo like a middle-aged suburban housewife and/or God forbid, Fred the Furrier.

But since he considers himself a modern guy, you won't catch him saying horrible things about his wife in order to get you into the sack. For example, the old-fashioned Dan would have told you how he only stayed with her for the children, but that she was frigid, uncaring, unconcerned about his work, and that he grew over the years but she hadn't. He had to say those things about her to get you. But somewhere along the way (probably around 1973), we all got liberated, which not only gave women the right to work harder but allowed men to work less. Now he doesn't even have to make up clever lies to get you into bed. Also (in spite of all that extra work), we started believing the popular notion (begun no doubt by married men) that there were so many more of us than there were of them that we'd better take what we could get and learn to make soufflé for breakfast.

This was like a bonus from heaven for Dan. Now he could fool around and only have to make up stories *for* his wife and not *about* her. Therefore, he won't tell you he's about to: 1) leave her; 2) marry you.

## What You're Like Now . . .
## What You Were Like Then

Everyone knows that fooling around with married men is deadly, particularly on your birthday, his birthday, Christmas, Thanksgiving, Guy Fawkes day, Memorial Day, or any other holiday. The only time you can be assured of seeing him is during Tuesday afternoon trysts, when he says he's with clients, or Thursday night liaisons, when he tells his wife that he's playing racquet ball. (We'll get to that later.)

Even though everyone knows that he's deadly, millions of women foolishly think that they will be able to handle it and that they are different and therefore immune. Unfortunately these same women are the very ones to start doodling their *first* names with his *last* name as soon as he boards the 11:15 back to Larchmont. Now, call me extreme, but that doesn't sound immune to me. In reality, the only difference between the woman who is stuck with Dan now and the woman who was stuck with this kind of guy in your mother's day was that she got better presents.

## Trysting the Night Away

You will meet Dan and somehow end up having a drink with him. If you haven't met him at work, you might also meet him at a singles bar, where he will pretend to be single. If you suspect that he entered with false ID, ask him for his phone number when he asks you for yours, and say that you'll be out of town, but you can call him the next night or so. If he gives you his work number and *not* his home number, he's married or living with someone. It's that simple.

The best way to spot him is that he has a commuter rail pass stuck in his wallet when he pays for the drinks. He also is probably carrying in his briefcase a duplicate of the shirt he left home wearing this morning. After all, it wouldn't do to go home with lipstick on his collar, now would it? If his wife notices the shirt in his briefcase, he tells her that he still takes his favorite shirts to his favorite Chinese laundry in the city. Somehow, even though he would die before he ever would go to the dry cleaners in the burbs, she buys this story of his inexplicable loyalty to a Chinese laundry.

## What He Knows That You Don't Know If You Are His Girlfriend

1. He will never use the Cashmere Bouquet soap in the motel bathroom when he showers. Motels are the only places in the world that have the stuff, and an alert wife can smell it at 100 paces . . . or less.

2. His thoughtful perfume presents to you happen to match his thoughtful observance of his wife's favorite fragrance. She thinks she's smelling herself on him when he comes home.

81

3. If all else fails, and he *has* used the Cashmere Bouquet and you have *refused* to use the perfume, he will stop in a bar on his way home, order a Scotch and pour a good part of it on himself. He might even ask someone to blow smoke on him. That's because "getting drunk with the boys" is less life threatening than fooling around with some dame on the at-home scoreboard.

4. Yes, he probably will have a command performance with his wife when he gets home, just so that she doesn't accuse him of fooling around. God knows (she thinks), he'd be too exhausted to make love to two women in one night.

## What He Knows That You Don't Know If You Are His Wife

1. The switchboard of the hotel he's staying at on business really does accept incoming calls.

2. The reason your joint American Express bill goes directly to his office now really doesn't have anything to do with his expense account. It's because they send receipts with the bill, and these stubs have caused more men to pay more alimony and child support than all the private detectives on earth.

3. He will leave on a business trip one night early, and spend that night with "her." "Her" will be very grateful, which is why you will probably never get rid of the creep. She's grateful and you're not.

4. If she pressures him into taking her away for a weekend, he will concoct some insane story about going to a sales conference or on a hunting/fishing trip where he can't be

reached. If you find evidence that he didn't go, he will have proof that he did.

5. It's not true that the reason he comes home from racquet ball with still-pressed, unsweaty clothes in his gym bag is because they have a laundress on staff at the court.

6. Yes, he *can* make love to two different women on one single night. If even *he* thinks the effort will kill him, he will come in the door holding his stomach and claiming it must be something he ate.

## What to Do if You Are His Wife

1. Get a good lawyer before he does.

2. Tell him that you are interested in investing, and you want a parking lot of your own.

3. Switch your perfume if you want to be sure.

4. Take up with his best friend since college the second you have a separation agreement.

5. Charge at least two thousand dollars on your joint American Express card (the one with the receipts that go directly to his office) for lingerie and never wear one stitch for him. Leave it around, however.

6. After he moves in with "her," drop the kids, the turtle, the dog with oozing sores, and the kids' laundry off at his new love nest before you go away on vacation by yourself.

## The Reality of the Relationship if You're the Girlfriend

Somehow against all your better instincts, you find that you *are* involved with him. Even though you swore that you were just in it for the sex, and until something better came along it would be fun. Besides, you thought, having a secret lover would make you more confident and sexier, and that's when other men would flock around like flies. For some insane reason, this equation only works when you are involved with an available man. When you are involved with an available man, all you meet are wonderful other available men. When you are involved with a married man, all you meet are other women who are involved with married men. And, let's face it, everyone else is busy Christmas Day (except you).

Now, of course there are advantages to this involvement. For one thing, it's easier than taking a chance with an available man and then getting rejected. Let me explain: When you are involved with a Dan, you can easily convince yourself that it's not that he doesn't *want* to be with you on Christmas, it's just that he *can't* be with you on Christmas. If an available man suddenly takes a powder on Christmas and heads for the Bahamas without you, then it's pretty clear that drinking hot mulled wine with you on Christmas Eve isn't his first choice. If Dan ends up with wife and kiddies in the Bahamas on Christmas, however, he says it was against his will. He will be tortured while skin diving, snorkeling, drinking out of coconuts, and motor scootering around without you. He would, he says with his eyes, much rather be drinking hot mulled wine with you. He's lying. And so are his eyes.

### Dealing the Cards and Winning the Game

First, admit to yourself that he's probably not going to leave his hearth and home for you and even if he does, chances are good that he won't discover what freedom is like until after you've nursed him through his divorce.

There are two approaches that can make your life less miserable. The first is to date every other man in the world, and only see him when it's convenient for you. Drive him looney with your schedule and don't reserve Thursday nights for him because that's the night he can get away the easiest. Send yourself flowers, and buy yourself cocktail dresses and leave them on hangers over your bedroom door. *If* he gets angry and accuses you of cheating on him, laugh in his face. Don't—I repeat—*don't ever let him get you somehow into a monogamous relationship. This relationship is not monogamous. He's got a wife.*

### Only Women with No Self-Esteem Whatsoever Take Up with Married Men Who Are Also Poor

The other alternative is to refine your bad taste in men to men who can afford to cheat. Only rich men should have the audacity to cheat on their wives. All others should be beaten about the head and neck. Now, provided that you really like the guy in the first place (we're not talking about Mayflower Madam sleaze here), tell him you are interested in the bond market, and learning about investing. Let him invest his money for you, and when he wants to buy you fur coats tell him to buy you a parking lot instead. You mustn't be ashamed to accept presents . . . after all, if he were your boyfriend and he didn't have a wife, you two would certainly be exchanging presents. Then when he finally admits that he can never leave his wife for you or anyone, you can cry all the way to the parking lot to pick up your weekly receipts. It only makes sense.

## What's It All About, Ralphie?

It's all about getting him before he gets you. He is a playboy who hides behind domesticity. He wants his cake and to eat you too. Well, that's not the way you should let it be. You certainly deserve better than that, don't you? First of all, he's not nice for cheating on his wife. That's a really low-life betrayal of someone who is also supposed to be the closest person in the world to him. And secondly, if he cheats once, he cheats twice and so on and so forth. There really is only one thing to do. Leave him and marry someone else. If you think you don't deserve a man to call your own, you won't get one. If you think you deserve a man who belongs to someone else, chances are good that's what you'll get.

## BEST OF BREED

### Dan, Dan the Married Man

Most Chutzpa:
## HENRY THE EIGHTH

For Inventing a Whole New Religion
So He Could Cheat on His Wife

Second Place Chutzpah:
## ROBERT KENNEDY

For Taking Marilyn off His Brother's
Back and Assuming the Burden
Himself

Every Which Way but Loose Award:
## ANYONE IN THE BRAT PACK

They Are Particularly Famous for
Trying to Score with Anything That
Moves Including All Industrial
Machinery

Does Rice Come With the
Dinner Award
## GARY HART

**IMPOSSIBLE MAN #9**

## Sincerely Yours

Sincerely Yours is just . . . well . . . too sincere. He is the man you may have met at a No Nukes, Live Aid, or Green Peace rally that you attended in the hopes of bringing about nuclear disarmament, and failing that in the hopes of meeting a man. Look, you never know who you might meet at one of these things. After all, it could have been Tom Robbins or David Bowie. But it wasn't.

Sincerely might also have been your professor in college, your est trainer, the best Jungian on the block, or even your acting coach. But whatever he is and wherever you met him, you can be sure of one thing—he is older than you and too dangerous to be doing so much good for the world while wreaking havoc among the poorly karmaed women who get snared in his guitar strings. Just rest assured that he is in a position of power relative to yours when you meet.

Sincerely is a roamer, and he may tell you that he began his career in the Peace Corps in India. He swears he hung out with Mother Teresa, among others. (It was a long time ago, so she was only Daughter Teresa then.) Right off you should know that he is an intellectual groupie. And fortunately or unfortunately, Sincerely is becoming something of an endangered species, which is about as tragic as finding out that there are only four slugs left in North America. The reason that he is going the way of the platypus is that most young men would rather learn to play the stock market than the acoustic guitar these days.

This man is usually too poor to logically afford to be so sincere, or he is too wealthy to be taken seriously. But no matter which, he is tortured. He is also metaphysical, vegetarian (or at least red-meatless), and open-minded (as long as it's left, liberal, and slightly illegal). If he has a profession, surely it will be firmly grounded in the land that time forgot . . . like the sixties. This man can actually throw pots, be into leather (not bondage), and/or teach Marxism in the Twenty-First Century at a liberal college. And even though he acts poor, somehow or other he seems always to have enough money to trek to places like Nepal, though not enough to expect you not to go Dutch on dates.

### The Women Who Drive Him Wild

Sincerely likes young women, or more specifically, he likes young women to like him. (Half his age is a good starting point.) The only exception to that rule: If he's stayed with the same woman for many years, and she is no longer half his age, she is either more sensitive than he could ever dream of being, or she is so insensitive that she never noticed all the college-age women he brought home to dinner . . . probably because she was out sneaking around herself.

## Why He Is the Way He Is

Sincerely was brought up in a well-to-do family that taught him that being smart and sensitive were the most important virtues one could attain. He was also taught that smart boys either got good grades or had insensitive teachers, and that superior boys would opt for home ec. over auto shop, would rather paint pictures than paint walls, and would rather eat something once attached to the ground than eat anything once attached to legs. This means that his women get to fix the flats, paint the kitchen, and eat brown-rice casseroles.

While other young boys broke their arms falling out of trees and playing baseball, he broke his heart over man's inhumanity to man. Unfortunately he never thought about man's inhumanity to the woman who might someday show up as his unlucky wife and/or lover.

Sincerely attended good schools, no question. Good, liberal-education schools to be more precise. He was pegged at seven as a creative genius, and learned to write rather than to spell. And even though he is a proud believer in women's rights, he just can't help but notice women's wrongs . . . especially the women he's involved with.

## Sincerely and No Man's Land

Sincerely has never had, nor does he ever wish to have, any kind of macho male bonding. In other words, he's never had a beer-drinking buddy.

The only time he ever got in a bar fight, as a matter of fact, was quite recently when someone accused Bob Dylan of secretly being E.T.'s voice-over in the movie. He's tortured that he didn't write "We Are the World," even though he swears he was just about to when the song hit the airwaves. He attended "Live Aid," "Band Aid," "Farm Aid," and would have attended "Kool Aid" if they'd held one outside of Guyana. He found each "aid" concert lacking the "authenticity" of Woodstock.

If you've ever made it into his sphere of women, you'll probably notice right off that you aren't the only woman who is drawn to him. In fact, the numbers are legion. He's brilliant, insightful, and a ladies' man. And you won't realize that men stay away from him as much as women stick to him until it's regrettably too late. Up till then you thought that they (meaning every other man in the world) were just jealous of him. You're wrong. Regular men just don't trust any guy who eats soyburgers publicly.

## His Way with You

Sincerely loves life. He says. Sincerely can cry at the birth of a child. He says. Sincerely will make you feel like the world's luckiest woman to be the one who has snagged him. He implies. He has been Rolfed, est-blessed, re-birthed but not re-born. And his patterns in a relationship reflect all of this. Therefore they are predictable. He will be:

91

1) enchanted     2) enchanting     3) intolerant
4) tortured.

And this, mind you, all in the course of one term with you.

Here's how it goes: You meet Sincerely. Perhaps you are a student in his Marxism in the Twenty-First Century class. All the women are drawn to his well-worn (expensive) tweedy jacket, his soft-soled shoes, his (yes, admit it!) pipe. Somehow, his eyes seem to rest on you a bit too much . . . a bit longer than the other women. Your boyfriend, who may even be in his class, calls him a wimp. You drop your boyfriend because he is insensitive and because he doesn't wear hush puppies. You can also no longer tolerate the fact that the old boyfriend goes around saying things like, "The only good Marx is a dead Marx . . . Groucho, Harpo, Chico, and Zeppo!" The old boyfriend took you to the movies; Sincerely takes you to film retrospectives. But he won't take you to a film retrospective until *after* he's slept with you. He implies. You believe. And you are wrong.

## The Courtship

Sincerely will start your relationship by being . . . as his name implies . . . "Sincerely Yours." He will bring you a single flower that he's picked on his way over. (You can forget large, showy, wonderfully tasteless floral arrangements from this one.) For some bizarre reason, you won't even have the decency to be ashamed to show your friends the one perfect tiger lily he found just for you (even if their apartments are sporting dozens of long-stemmed you-know-whats).

He will sit on the floor of your living room, drink wine, and eat brie. He will tell you about his stint in third-world countries doing good deeds. And for the first few months of your relationship he will be completely smitten with you, therefore *he* will make love to *you*. Then somehow, you end up even more smitten with him and *you* are the one who makes love to *him*. He talks in clichés, telling you how he has become obsessed with you . . . how tortured he was watching you from afar . . . never sure whether to approach you or to keep you as his fantasy. Here, then, dialog from your first date on . . .

### Date One: His Way

HE SAYS:   I don't know what it is that draws me to you like this.

HE MEANS: Look at those knockers!

### Date Two: His Way

HE SAYS:   No one understands me.

HE MEANS: She wants me.

### Six Months Later

HE SAYS:   You've upset me too much to spend the night.

HE MEANS: Watch it, honey, I don't get mad, I get going.

### Date One: Your Way

HE SAYS:   I don't know what draws me to you like this.

SHE SAYS: Ask me if I care.

## Date Two: Your Way

HE SAYS: No one understands me.

SHE SAYS: No, it's not true; I do. Did I tell you that I'm thinking of switching health clubs?

## Six Months Later: Your Way

HE SAYS: You've upset me, but can I still spend the night?

SHE SAYS: No, because you've upset me too much to spend the night. Besides I have to get up early to wash my sneakers.

HE SAYS: Huh?

## My Space or Yours

After your first date, he may take you home and leave you there. Alone. If you live in a big city, he may put you in a cab and kiss you sweetly on the cheek. He won't pay the driver, either. You sit there half-steaming . . . half-burning. And that brings us to . . .

Rule #1: Any man who makes you want to both strangle him *and* sleep with him after one date is trouble. Remember that.

He won't bring up "his space or yours" until you are frothing at the mouth. If that happens on date one, you *know* what you were doing.

## The Sincere Work Ethic: If It Hurts, It Must Be Right

He'll make you work for things. When he does finally bed down, you get the odd feeling that it was because he finally succumbed . . . not because he found you irresistible. This is simply not true. He does (or did) find you irresistible; you just never knew it. And admittedly, it's hard to feel irresistible while spending nights like a sixteen-year-old, making your friends drive you past his house—or worse—forcing these same friends under threat of death—yours—to call up and pretend to be selling subscriptions to *Boys' Life* just so you'll know if he's home.

Now, here comes the part that's hard to believe, but it's true. It's not that he hasn't found you desirable, it's just that it's hard for him to part with his first love . . . himself. He and his alter ego have spent many a wonderful night together; after all being a tortured, misunderstood, creative genius is tough work. It tires a guy out.

If you must have him to call your own, then be prepared to be more tortured, more misunderstood, and more of a creative genius than he—which is, of course, more hard work. Or simply be someone who shops for a living . . . someone who subscribes to the *National Enquirer* . . . someone who wears too-tight leather and appreciates him only as a sex object. Be unashamed and unafraid to use him and lose him. (You won't.)

Go home without spending the night, and never, ever say things like, "When will I see you again?" Or worse, "I've loved being with you . . . should I call you tomorrow?" Refrain. Refrain. Refrain. Let him think that the only way to make you notice him is to notice something about him that no one else had the nerve to notice before: sex. When he brings you the single flower, be prepared to stick it in a vase that you already have filled with a dozen long-stemmed roses. When he asks you if you love Rimbaud as much as he, ask him if he means Sylvester Stallone . . . or the poet who killed himself at age thirty-six in a French garret. Then shamelessly say you hope that he didn't mean the poet, because you hate tortured poets who kill themselves in garrets. Besides, as far as you're concerned the only Rambo worth listening to is Sylvester Stallone. Then immediately seduce him. Don't give him time to argue or look exasperated. And above all, manage to do all of this while looking smart as a whip. It's not that you don't know the difference between Rimbaud and Rambo, it's just that you think one is pretentious. Got it? (Even if you think it's the other one.)

## Sincerely Yours as Mate: Then and Now

Sincerely has probably been married at least once, and he probably has a child or two. If he does, he is tortured (or so he says) about not being with the kids. He gets teary-eyed when he talks about what it's been like living without his kids . . . even if they are *your* age by now. And there's a good chance that they will be. In fact, if Sincerely has been separated from his ex-wife and kids long enough, he may indeed push for marriage with you simply because he's ready to play the part of tweedy father to an infant.

Therefore, one can't help but be curious about how the children of his first family feel about seeing Dad suddenly carrying on about the wonders of fatherhood and infancy. And now that you think about it wasn't Sincerely one of the men who became semifamous once by finding his inner being by wearing beads, visiting gurus, going macrobiotic, and writing articles about the socioeconomic insanity of the nuclear family and monogamy?

I wonder if family number one was annoyed that when papa finally found himself, he was found with a whole new set of relatives? (Yours, to be precise.) And now that he's decided to be married to you, you may suddenly decide that you don't know what's worse, being with a man who refuses to give emotionally, or being with a man who refuses *not* to give emotionally . . . twenty-four hours a day! Everything becomes a chance to "share."

### Talk Is Cheap: His Way

HE SAYS:   I'd like to share with you how I feel about this dinner.

HE MEANS: When I say macrobiotic kosher cuisine, I don't mean pork roast and Tab.

HE SAYS:   I want to share my feelings about tonight and let you know that if you choose to find someone else attractive, well, I understand.

HE MEANS: Basically, I hate you.

### Talk Is Cheap: Your Way

SHE SAYS: *I'd* like to share with *you* how I feel about this dinner. From now on the only thing I make is reservations!

### Sincerely Yours as New Papa

Watch it . . . the child you raise may grow up to be Sincere! Sincerely papas seem to be turning (even as we speak) into the fanatical mothers of previous generations. They seem to be mother/fathers who (after they've given up being lover-boys to sophomores) now spend their days with their babies at places with names like "The Better Baby Institute." This ensures that their children can write in script, and speak French, before they reach one year of age. After you give birth, it is Sincerely who sees himself reflected in the greater glory of his genius-rated progeny. You point out to him that he left wifey number one because she was acting just like he's acting now! But he may in fact simply enjoy losing himself to the tasks of motherhood too much to ever give it up.

So stop revering him for grinding baby food and cutting cloth diapers. Remember, it's only a phase. After all, his grown children spent their childhoods with access to him only on visiting days.

So, after all of this, why would anyone *want* to have a meaningful relationship with this one? Because in his own pompous way, he can be wonderful. But only if you can teach him to laugh. He's never been taught that laughter isn't a sin, and that people will still take him seriously even if he *does* have a sense of humor. If he learns to laugh at himself first, he can be a prize you'll want to hold close forever. But if he doesn't, go buy some Ravi Shankar records and be prepared for a long, cold winter.

**BEST OF BREED**

**Sincerely Yours**

Best Domestic Version:
ALAN ALDA*

Best Sixties Version That Didn't
Convert Well in Any Other Decade:
TIMOTHY LEARY

JERRY RUBIN

WILLIAM KUNSTLER

JAMES BALDWIN

JESSE JACKSON

BOB DYLAN. BOB DYLAN. BOB
DYLAN.

"That Girl's" Boyfriend:
TED BISSELL

*A time machine is indicated for those of you who
like this kind of man . . . he's getting rarer by the
second.

**IMPOSSIBLE MAN #10**

# Awesomely Uncommitted Man

Awesome resembles many of the other impossibles in some uncontrollable ways. In fact, he can be the best and the worst of the lot. When you let him enter your life, you allow in a true erotic nightmare. Erotic because he can be very sexy and loving, and a nightmare because he never gets beyond the "going out" stage even if you've been going out for seventeen years. He can't help it, poor guy; he has a fear of engraved invitations. It runs in his family . . . his father sent one out once and got stuck with his mother. For life. His mother sent one out once and got stuck with a life sentence. Yeah, *they're* happy all right.

100

So early on he decided that a lifetime of bickering just so you could get laid on a regular basis by someone who got on your nerves and who probably hated sex (or why would she go to bed wearing goop on her face?) didn't make a whole lot of sense.

So now, you've got this prize and you completely believe that if you can just hang in there *long* enough you'll win him over and he'll be calling you up to discuss engraved invitations sooner or probably later. And you are wrong. Longevity breeds contempt with this one.

## Where He Breeds, What He Needs

Awesome knows no boundaries. He's been spotted all over the world, and is not indigenous to any climate. At all. He may not be hip, but he is in point of fact clean. He loves starched shirts, nice ties, and slacks with good creases. He is more yuppie than Jerry Rubin, if possible, and is probably as intellectually deep as ol' Jer, which means that if you scratch the surface you'll come up empty.

His insatiable passions are music and movies and the right equipment to play them on. He had the first VCR ever made and nearly went into cardiac arrest the first time he heard a compact disc. Therefore, you can find him at Radio Shack or Crazy Eddie's on any given night, in deep conversation with the salesmen who honestly care about finding him the perfect connecting wire widget. Or he may simply be browsing the amplifiers or buying obscure records that you've never heard of and, with any luck, never *will* hear of.

The local video store has a shrine in his name.

So does his favorite car dealer. That's his second favorite passion. He buys cars the way normal people buy groceries. He loves cars and always thinks he can find an even better car than the one he has. His car has a stereo system that sounds like a recording studio. Riding in his car is like being in other people's living rooms. Only cleaner.

### The Man With a Plan

His most distinguishing characteristic, however, is his unrivaled ability to make confirmed plans with his friends for all vacations, summers, and holidays years in advance, while being unable to make future plans with you that extend beyond the next fifteen minutes. If you say you'd like to plan to spend Memorial Day weekend together, he'll say something clever like "whatever." It makes no sense, but then, neither does he.

### Spotting an Awesomely Uncommitted Man

Awesome is likely to be spotted in any place that caters to singles and exceptionally clean people. So you might find him (when he's not at Crazy Eddie's) in a gourmet food shop, Chinese laundry, nouvelle cuisine restaurant, any Hampton except Lionel, Club Med, the cleaning aisle of the supermarket, in the best seat of an obscure classical or sixties rock concert, at the local exotic car dealership.

He wears jeans on the weekends and always has a great pair of sneakers on his feet. He is obsessed by his hair and always has a decent haircut that's never quite right. If he's losing his hair, it is to him the equivalent of having cancer. You are sure to find Minoxidil somewhere in his home, or in his bag if you are away together. He spends a great deal of time gently patting the top of his head in a bizarre manner. It's his way of testing to see if any more hair has come loose in the last three minutes.

He wears glasses and has tried contacts, and he is on a first-name basis with his eye doctor called Larry who's one of his Hampton housemates.

## Your First Date

He'll pick you up and take you somewhere nice. He's wearing an all-cotton starched shirt with French cuffs. He smells vaguely of Aramis or some other annoying shaving lotion. He'll drink either single malt Scotch or vodka, and will definitely order the pasta whatever it is. He'll be especially thrilled if they have gnocci on the menu. Don't even be tempted to ask what gnocci is.

## Your First Conversation

| | |
|---|---|
| HE SAYS: | I'd like to be married, have kids, the whole nine yards. I'm getting too old to be a bachelor . . . I'm ready to get married. |
| HE MEANS: | *If* I found someone who looked like Christie Brinkley, took her clothes off as quickly as Debra Winger in a movie, raised children with the skill of Mrs. Cleaver, had the pa- |

tience of Mother Teresa, and could earn a hundred grand or more in a nice part-time job, I'd marry her in a minute.

YOU SAY: Oh, really?

YOU SHOULD HAVE SAID: If there's anything I don't want to be it's married. Why do I only meet men who want to get married?

HE SAYS: Huh?

HE MEANS: This is a new one for me!

YOU SAY: Is the food good here?

Completely ignoring his lies about wanting to get married makes him totally insane. Every woman he's ever been out with hears the wedding march upon the utterance of these magic words and is sure that he means her, he thinks. (Therefore, if you disregard all his nonsense it will make him—if not mad for you—at least anxious enough to keep calling. Lucky you.)

If the wedding talk hasn't budged you, he will switch tactics to show you that he's a man with *plans*. Plans are his life. He already has plans to take a house in the Hamptons with the same group of survivors that he's housed with for the last five summers. He plans to summer with them this year and next, and by the third summer, he will have accrued enough sick time and vacation time to take a month and a half off, at which time he will take a house in Spain with four of his housemates from the Hamptons. He's found out that you can get a cleaning lady in Spain for four dollars a day, including laundry! This may in fact be the most telling part of his whole litany. Because, like it or not, cleaning women mean a great deal to him. Cleanliness and order mean a great deal to him. He is anal to the point of turning it into a religious experience.

His present cleaning lady is the most important woman in his life. She's competent, she's amusing, she's organized, she starches his sheets. He's happy when she's there. She makes no demands and all he has to do is give her a bonus at Christmas. He doesn't even have to make a pretense of going into Gucci's.

He would like, in theory at least, to be married. But in reality he sees no need for it, although he does like to have a steady girlfriend he can see (sleep with) a predictable number of days a week and probably on Saturday night. He would like to have relationships with women that could stay on that basis forever. Why spoil the fun? he thinks. And besides, if you're married, you have to get a station wagon.

Here's the kicker: He may have even been married before. What did she have that you don't have? Him, when he was young enough *not* to know that he didn't want to be married.

## What He Likes to Do with You

- Make love and then roll over so fast you'd think he had ball bearings on his back.

- Go shopping for stereo equipment for his apartment.

- Go to the movies and out for dinner on the weekends.

- Keep your relationship in that gray limbo-land for as long as he's comfortable with it, which could be forever or maybe next week.

- Go for rides with his kids and take them places.

## What He Likes to Do
## Without You

- Attend family functions (his).

- See old girlfriends for dinner and lunch.

- Have dinner with his parents and siblings and *their* spouses or dates.

- Go to his best friend's wedding in another state.

- Escort other women to black tie functions as though you were his mistress and he was secretly keeping you, when as far as you know all you've ever gotten out of him is a Trivial Pursuit game to keep at your house.

- *Make plans.* While you aren't looking, he books a mountain-climbing course for every Sunday for three months, signs on for his share of the summer house, books his Club Med trip.

- Keep all of the above from you until each one is a fait accompli. When you get crazy and scream about being excluded, he'll say, "I thought you wouldn't enjoy it." Or, "I need some space to do my own things once in a while. I don't understand why you don't find things of your own to do. I'm not your social director." Then you'll have a huge fight, and somehow or other *you* end up apologizing.

## More Fun with Anal
## and Oral Roberts

He will probably never tell you he loves you, although there *is* one Awesome species in particular that says it right away and says it constantly for a few months before he tapers off. Don't get excited by all that love talk. He very rarely makes the leap over into commitment.

If he's the more readily available type, you will go out with him for months, see each other on many weekends, and never hear anything like "I love you." He will actually have the nerve after seeing you for a year to scream out his *fondness* for you in the clinches. Maddening *and* embarrassing is what it is.

He slips out of commitment talk like a greased swimmer out of a pool. The more you push the worse it gets. If you push too much he'll leave, which would be okay, if you honestly could see him for what he is, which you simply will not be able to do until he's ancient history.

You attempt to take him for dinner at happily married friends' homes. He brings the wine and doesn't get the setup. At all. Instead of seeing blessed domesticity, he says they look like they live in student digs. See what marriage does to people? Instead of envying them their lovely children, he gets you alone and says that he hates out-of-control children who use the floor to lie around on, and how much longer does he have to endure this, anyway?

## How He Differs from All the Rest

Unlike most of the others, he is definitely *there*. If he says he'll call you on Monday, he'll call you on Monday. He doesn't disappear and not call again. He simply never allows the relationship to go beyond a certain point. You'll never know whether you're going to see him on the weekends. He seems to go away on weekends a lot. But where? And with whom? Through osmosis, you get the feeling that to ask would be unpleasant, embarrassing, and/or infuriating. He may or may not lie about his whereabouts, and besides he sees you a lot. He says.

## What You Will Never Know About Him. Ever.

- Whether or not he's seeing other women while he's seeing you. You think he's not, but who knows?

- If his parents hate you and that's why you've only met them once.

- If the rumors are true that one of his ex-girlfriends is really in the loony bin because of him.

- If there really was some woman in his past that made every other pale by comparison.

- If he really did want to marry her and she broke his heart.

- How much money he earns, has, or spends.

## What You Will Always Know About Him

- He has neices and nephews that he spends a lot of time with.

- He has siblings that he spends a lot of time with.

- His brother or his brother-in-law is his best friend.

- He has dinner with ex-girlfriends a lot.

- He's very close to his family.

- They want to marry him off.

- It's the only concession he won't make.

## How to Save Your Sanity

There's not much you can do, aside from making your own plans. He admires that. When he asks you out, refrain from accepting from time to time. He won't disappear. Don't ever come out and say it, but allude to another relationship.

Shock him by planning your vacations and summer weekends without him. If at all possible, run into him where he summer-shares. If at all possible, have a hunk on your arm. Whenever you go out to dinner with Awesomely Uncommitted, get up every fifteen minutes to call your answering machine. It will make him nervous. Call your machine from his car phone and make him berserk.

Go out with as many other men as you can find, so that you don't become obsessed. It will help you to deal with him if he knows he's not coming from a position of power.

Plan to attend your family gatherings without him and tell him that you're going. It might not change the way he deals with you, but at least he'll wonder why you don't ask him. It never occurs to him that it has nothing to do with him not asking *you* to attend his.

When he asks you what's going on, tell him you adore him but are just so busy you don't know what to do first. You may not win him, but at least he'll get dented.

# The Awesomely Uncommitted Man as Husband

## The Awesomely Uncommitted Man as Daddy

Now although it's nearly impossible to get these guys married off, they do from time to time sire a brood or two. Out of sheer desperation, however, many women foolishly revert back to pre-sexual-revolution tactics. They think that when all else fails, get pregnant—and they are wrong. Awesome likes kids. He just doesn't like marriage. And this maneuver will not tie him to *you*, it will simply tie him to his *children*. Which in turn will tie *you* down. Anyone who has children without benefit of husband gets to spend many nights alone with children who have 108° temperatures.

That's not to say he won't help support them, attend functions, and have a good time with them. It gives him the best of all possible worlds. He gets to be a father without having to be a husband. His kids adore him, because he is like the candy man. He's there for all the fun things. He teaches them how to buy stereos, and they love riding around in his latest car, with his latest girlfriend.

His parents consider the whole thing a big disgrace and don't really consider the children grandchildren because they aren't *family*. Huh? If you can't help yourself and you must at least try this pregnancy test of true love, then at least have the good sense to believe him when he says he's happy about the baby but he doesn't want to get married. He means it.

**BEST OF BREED**

## The Most Awesomely
## Uncommitted Men
## in History:

Earliest Known Version:
ONE MILLION B.C.:

### ADAM
of Eve Fame.
He might have been crazy about
her . . . but he didn't marry her, even
*after* she had the kids.

The Most Overextended Man in a
Military Capacity
195 B.C.

### HANNIBAL

Figured out how to cross the Alps on
elephants and kept making Punic wars
just so he didn't have to get involved
in a meaningful relationship at home.

# The Awesomely Uncommitted Hall of Fame Prime Example of What Marriage Can Do to a Guy: 1079–1142

## PETER ABELARD*

*After a quick but exciting marriage to Heloise, Peter (who took the time between women to found the University of Paris) found himself without, er, the right stuff to continue being a playboy, thanks to Heloise's uncle and his squad of goons. Although she was perfectly willing to take him back with or without the right stuff (or any stuff, for that matter), he was pissed off (literally) and punished her for her undying devotion to him by becoming a monk and convincing her to become a nun. He continued to be Awesomely Uncommitted throughout his life by paying her visits and pretending that he wanted to quit being a monk so he could marry her again. Rumor has it that she could have given Mrs. Havisham a run for her money in waiting for a groom to make good on his word.

## New World Heroes

How Many More Blondes Are Gonna
Fall for that Story? Award

**ROD STEWART**

(Special note: If any blonde will ever
capture him alive, it's Kelly Emberg.)

Listen . . . About Marriage Only
Being a Piece of Paper . . . Award

**SAM SHEPARD**

**MIKHAIL BARYSHNIKOV**

**RYAN O'NEAL**

Now I Mean, Is That Nice? Promising
the Woman and Then Running Off
with Jackie Kennedy Like That?
Award

**ARISTOTLE ONASSIS**
(For His Treatment of Maria Callas)

## Women in the News Awards

The Only Three Women in the World
Smart Enough to Outfox
the Best of the Best

### FARRAH FAWCETT

"I Have No Intention of Ever
Marrying You" Award for Bravery in
the Face of the Odds.

### JESSICA LANGE

For actually refusing Mikhail
Baryshnikov *after* the baby was born
and then running off to live happily
ever after in the desert with Sam
Shepard and refusing him too. Wow.
The woman should be in a shrine
she's so good.

"Are You Kidding? Without the
Benefit of Marriage? Never! Award."

### JACKIE KENNEDY ONASSIS

*Blue Ribbon* for getting the world's
second richest and first most
Awesomely Uncommitted Man (Jack
Kennedy) to chase her like crazy and
then beg to marry her and then leave
her all his money. *Blue Ribbon* for
getting the world's richest and second
most Uncommitted Man, (Aristotle
Onassis) to leave his diva and chase
her like crazy and beg to marry her
and then leave her a huge chunk of
his money.

# PART TWO

Impossible
Lovers,
Mothers,
and
Others

# Are You Expecting Too Much from Love?

**H**ere it is at last, the final word on whether your expectations about love, loving, and lovers are too high . . . or too low. Do you expect that impossible man of yours to "walk a fine line between man and superman"? Well, put Nietzsche aside and take this simple quiz. It may change your life! At least it will tell you whether you are doomed to love impossible men all your natural life.

### A Quick Quiz for Women Who Are Drawn to Impossible Men

1. The Men You Date:

    A) Wear stethoscopes or they wear nothing at all

    B) Work in a variety of fields including weaving, leather working, and three-card monte stings

    C) You don't know since you are an abbess.

2. You Like a Man Who Is:

    A) Rich

    B) Sincere, kind, and empathetic

    C) Not in a coma

3. Books Are an Important Part of Your Life. To Make a Relationship Work, Your Man Must:

    A) Own a publishing company

B) Be good in bed

C) It doesn't matter, you can always teach him to read

4. You Are a Real Athlete, So It's Important for "Mr. Right" to:

A) Be rich

B) Own, or know someone who owns, a jogging suit

C) Be alive

5. You Believe that Good Sex in a Relationship:

A) Can be found outside of the relationship if he's got enough money

B) Is a myth

C) Good what?

6. Music Is Your Passion. Your Man Should:

A) Own RCA

B) Know that scales are more than things that grow on fish

C) Be an aficionado of elevator music

7. You Love Children. Your Ideal Man:

A) Should be willing to buy you some

B) Knows someone who has one

C) Should be allowed to cross by himself

8. Communication Is the Backbone of Every Good Relationship. Your Ideal Man Should:

A) Own AT&T

B) Know how to use both a dial and a push-button phone

C) Be somewhat familiar with the English language

9. Affection Is Important to You. You Look For:

A) A man who has learned to kiss without touching your hair and makeup

B) A man who has a working knowledge of Eric Segal's *Love Story*

C) A man

10. Your Parents Should Like Him, Too. They Will, If He:

A) Wears a stethoscope, owns RCA, AT&T, and a publishing company, is rich, and can kiss without touching you

B) Doesn't wear the *Daily News* for shoes

C) Breathes

### The Answers

If you chose mostly "A" answers, you are truly regal in your princess-like ways, my dear, and your aims are right on the mark. The more impossible the man, the more he will yearn to please you, and for sure you will get everything you've ever wanted.

If, however, you chose mostly "B" answers, your aims are off kilter, and you will spend countless hours crying to your shrink and your mother. Modify those demands a bit! If you forget the kind, loving, and empathetic stuff and go for the dough, you may yet find your impossible ideal.

121

If you chose mostly "C" answers, you don't deserve to have any man—impossible or not—to call your own. You must learn to be less demanding or more demanding. I recommend that you get out of the convent and into the castle as soon as possible.

# The Good, the Bad, and the Ugly

**Impossible Men and
Their Mothers We've Known and . . .**

## The WASP Mother

THE GOOD: He asks you to spend a weekend at his parents' country home.

THE BAD: His parents are there, and his mother's name is Bebe.

THE UGLY: His mother has never even heard of cellulite, and you've got the market cornered. To make matter worse, she's just asked you to join them for doubles.

## The Jewish Mother

THE GOOD: You're invited for Rosh Hashanah.

THE BAD: You wish them a hearty and happy Roshamon.

THE UGLY: You get one matzo in your matzo ball soup, and *it* lands on his mother's lace tablecloth.

## The Italian Mother

THE GOOD: His mother personally calls to invite you for Sunday dinner.

THE BAD: She has pictures of his wedding to his former wife all over the house.

THE UGLY: There's a picture of Mrs. X-wife and children with a votive candle burning next to your spot at the dinner table.

## The Irish Mother

THE GOOD: He asks you to meet his mother for dinner.

THE BAD: On Good Friday.

THE UGLY: His mother doesn't show up because she is at the rectory intimidating a priest.

## The Preppy Mother

THE GOOD: You're off for a weekend of skiing with his family at their lodge.

THE BAD: You don't know a pole from a ski.

THE UGLY: His mother asks Chip (or Skip or Bret) where you normally "winter." He says your apartment.

## The Doctor's Mother

THE GOOD: His mother is in town for the weekend and is dying to meet you.

THE BAD: She looks as though she might, when she does.

THE UGLY: She asks him what the first signs of shock are.

## The Lawyer's Mother

THE GOOD: His mother accepts an invitation for dinner at your house.

THE BAD: She falls over the cat, into the casserole, and asks her son to sue you.

THE UGLY: He does. And Oedipus rests.

## The Rich Man's Mother

THE GOOD: She's happy that you two are getting married.

THE BAD: She insists on a prenuptial agreement.

THE UGLY: The lawyer's *fee* is her wedding present.

## The Poor Man's Mother

THE GOOD: She's happy that you two are getting married.

THE BAD: She insists on a prenuptial agreement.

THE UGLY: The lawyer's *name* is her wedding present.

## The Good Boy's Mother

THE GOOD: He's finally agreed to let you meet his family after living with you for two years.

THE BAD: After dinner, his mother insists that you sit in the backseat of the car with her.

THE UGLY: They drop him off first . . . at their house.

## The Sensitive Man's Mother

THE GOOD: He's decided that he's finally in the "right space" to let you meet his mother.

THE BAD:   She's late because she was out getting Rolfed.

THE UGLY:  They spend the entire night crying over his inability to find his perfect mantra.

## Your Mother

THE GOOD:  She likes him.

THE BAD:   She makes him her special meat loaf.

THE UGLY:  He never calls you again. You hear he's run off to become a shepherd.

# Blind Dates From Hell!

## Nightmare Blind Dates with Impossible Men (Where everything that can *go wrong* will *go wrong)*

In your quest to find a prince, you will have to kiss many impossible men, on many a mondo bizarro occasion. Why? Let's be honest here, some people actually *do* meet the loves of their lives on blind dates. I have never personally met anyone who has, but I once heard of someone who did. So you have to give it a shot now and then. But you can be pretty sure you're with a frog who'll turn more impossible than princely if any of the following occur:

1. He says that he called the restaurant, and they don't accept reservations.

2. When you arrive, they tell you that you can't have a table without a reservation.

3. They make him put *their* tie over *his* I♥N.Y. tee shirt.

4. Only the waiters and your date speak French, and your date looks quite shocked at your lack of basic canard.

5. Everyone—including the waiters—laughs when he orders his entrée.

6. He discovers too late that his dinner will consist of one plate of French fries, so he quickly orders steak tartare. Rare.

7. He is forced to skip dessert for fear that it will turn out to be leg of lamb.

8. You hear a disgusting noise that isn't coming from your body.

9. You hear a disgusting noise that is.

10. Everyone, including the people at the next table, laughs when your date orders the wine.

11. The maitre d' comes by your table to ask if you could possibly hurry up because someone is waiting for your table. The place is more than half-empty.

12. You only have a five-dollar bill in your purse to tip the rest-room attendant, and your date says it's too large for him to break.

13. You return from the rest room trailing a large swath of toilet paper on your shoe, and your date joins everyone at the next table in a laugh fest.

14. His credit card is rejected. You offer yours and everyone, including the people at the next table, laughs.

15. They don't take credit cards at all, and you have fifteen dollars between you.

16. He asks you if you fool around, and when you say no, he looks at the bill and says, "Let's see, you had the glazed carrots, didn't you?"

17. As you are leaving the restaurant, the waiter holds out his tip with a look of disgust and asks you why you didn't enjoy your dinner. Out loud.

# The Impossible Man's
# Sexist Checklist

Every impossible man has all the answers. They know, for example, why we won't have a nuclear war, why old Austin Healys are better than new Jaguars, and why women behave the way that they do. Every Impossible Dream Man knows, too, that:

### All Men

Want a girl just like the girl that married dear old Dad, just so that they can leave underwear, socks, and wet towels on the bed, knowing full well that this action will not cause a stroke and the imminent death of the girl just like the girl.

### All Women

Want a boy just like the boy that married dear old Mom, so that they can stop feeling guilty about not wanting to wear loose cotton underwear and pyjamas with feet. Unfortunately if one marries a boy too much like the boy, one may have to spend an eternity with panty hose on. Loose cotton underwear can be held up in no other way. Therefore, he is sexy rather than kind.

### All Men

Believed their mothers when they said, "Why buy a cow when milk is so cheap?" as they were about to go and fool around in the backseat of a '67 Ford. They, therefore, will never forgive a woman if she does, and they will never forgive a woman if she doesn't.

## All Women

Refused to believe their mothers when they said, "Why buy a cow when milk is so cheap?" as they were about to go and fool around in the backseat of a '67 Ford. They therefore will never forgive a man who does, and they will never forgive his mother if he can't.

## All Men

Secretly yearn to be Mickey Mantle. And that is the only reason that they leave sports on *all* the time. They really believe that all of that cheering in the background of their lives is for their ability to read the Sunday *Times* while eating a Ring Ding. The Impossible Man happens to know that it's really only *true* in his case.

## All Women

Secretly yearn for the hated roar of the cheering crowd coming out of the TV set. Since they aren't watching, they believe that all of that cheering is for their great good fortune in capturing such a prize.

## All Men

Are thrilled with the fact that they are toilet trained. This is evidenced by various digestion announcements, and by the smug looks often associated with trips to the bathroom. He, on the other hand, is only proud of his great prowess with women, and that's why other men will never match up.

## All Women

Have a biological need to make beef stew for a man. He swears that he once scratched and sniffed an ardent feminist and smelled beef stock.

## All Men

Want to live in the Bloomingdale's catalog, which you may have noticed, never includes small children who invariably get fevers of 109° and then come downstairs and throw up on the life-style flokati.

## All Women

Who have children, have children who eat Bloomingdale's catalogs, throw up on life-style flokatis, and make disgusting noises whenever it can cause the greatest amount of embarrassment.

# The Impossible Woman As Bride

## How to Become Post-Deb of the Year

If you are in love with a charming, dashing, clever, social-climbing type of Impossible Man who you are afraid will break your heart, you're in trouble. What you obviously do not know, although I've certainly tried to warn you, is that in order not to get your heart broken by a charming, dashing, clever, social-climbing Impossible Man you must be a charming, dashing, clever, social-register type yourself. This is the reason that all those women get all these men to marry them. These men in turn spend the rest of their lives repenting at leisure for not having married you. They have their post-deb, and you have a broken heart.

Here then, to cut through all the red tape involved in a messy Impossible Man breakup, is a secret list that was snatched out of the Joan & David pump of a lady who lunches. (Don't laugh . . . do *you* get to have lunch for a living?)

### The Ideal Post-Deb

1. Must have been "presented" and come out successfully without ever having come.

2. No matter what her background, she has passed for WASP.

3. Must have friends with first names like Spencer, Muffin, Ceezee, and Chat.

4. Wears Adolfo dresses and sling-back shoes with various fruits on the front for summer, low-heeled Guccis for winter.

5. Has gone to Miss Porter's. (It doesn't count if anyone in her family ever worked *as* a porter.)

6. Once had a job as a fund raiser but gave it up because of the pressure.

7. Thinks everyone is just too cute.

8. Gets her hair done in a fame mane every week by Monsieur Mark.

9. If she has a child, he is very proper, and never breaks out, breaks things, or picks his nose.

10. The woman knows her linens.

11. Her day is just too overloaded what with nail appointments, charity functions, opera-committee meetings, and small talk.

12. "Suzy" calls her "Babs."

13. The woman has no rhythm.

14. She has the uncanny ability to convince everyone that gold Italian rococo furniture is tasteful in her apartment and hilariously gauche everywhere else.

15. She knows the precise minute that it became unfashionable to order rack of lamb and became fashionable to order something nouvelle cusine.

16. She has never seen an iceberg lettuce.

17. Belongs to a club called doubles.

18. Plays singles.

# Avoiding
# "Fat-Girl-Without-a-Date-
# for-the-Prom"
# Behavior

Fat-Girl-Without-a-Date-for-the-Prom behavior truly gets on my nerves. This is the kind of behavior that makes you take the most desperate actions and do the most life-humiliating things.

In this type of mind-set, you immediately become hundreds of pounds overweight the minute the man you crave doesn't call. You absolutely know that he'll never call, and that you'll never, in fact, have another date with *any*one ever again. You begin to cower and pout and whine and generally behave in ways that make everyone hate you. In other words, like the fat girls in your graduating class who didn't have dates for the you know what.

Once you get into Fat-Girl-Without-a-Date-for-the-Prom syndrome, you will do things like send the man of your dreams (who hasn't called you back) nauseating "sensitivity" or cutesy greeting cards. You will find yourself calling your best friend at 3:00 A.M. to ask her to make wrong-number calls to his house. You will make shameless hang-up calls. You will act like everytime you enter McDonald's they have to up the "billions-sold" sign. In short, you act like you need a size 22½ prom gown, even though you'll go to the prom alone and it's your father who'll be buying you the wrist corsage.

This is a natural-response trigger mechanism that happens whenever the guy you've had a great time with doesn't call back. Depending on your self-image, it can happen anywhere from one day to one week later. It is genetically programmed to occur to every woman except Pia Zadora, and it's something that happened even before telephones were invented. In those days women would sit by a wall where a telephone, if it had been invented, would have been. They would stare at the wall and say, "Why doesn't he call?" At this point someone would point out to her that he was unable to call because telephones weren't invented yet, and she'd have to go sit by the mailbox and humiliate herself in front of the mailman. And even though we no longer have to show our grief and longing to the mailman, we *have* invented new and exciting ways to act like "Fat Girl."

Here, then, are several surefire ways to avoid making an ass of yourself or at least of not appearing as though you needed a half-size prom gown . . . pronto!

### Emergency First Aid: How to Not Send Cute Cards When He Hasn't Called and Other Desperate Measures

Let's face it, pretending that you don't care in spite of a spate of magazine articles that tell you to simply move on to the next one when this one doesn't call you back, is next to impossible. Most women have found solace in the Hallmark store. There amidst "Happy Birthday to My Favorite Aunt" and the condolence cards sit the sensitive cards . . . and worse, the cute cards. The sensitive cards say things like "Seeing You Was Close to My Thoughts" and other completely inane and insane phrases. They make no sense unless you are desperate, and then they seem to be the only things besides Country and Western songs that *do* make any sense.

Worse even than these maudlin pieces of

cardboard with out-of-focus pictures of women wearing chiffon dresses and large hats in fields, are the cute cards. These completely insidious little numbers come complete with Peanuts characters (who've never been funny in the first place), Ziggy, and other cartoon characters, and are *designed* to appeal only to the extremely lonely, the desperate, and the extraordinarily obese.

Be honest here, would you actually send one of these cards to anyone else? No! You'd be ashamed to even sign your name. A lifetime of good taste and sensible judgment simply flies out the window in a crazed attempt to get the attention of the fool who hasn't called back.

It won't work. In fact, one male friend of mine says that it's a formula. When he doesn't call a woman back, he can almost calculate to the day just when the cute card will arrive in the mail. Up until he told me that, I honestly believed that I was the only woman who had found a friend at Hallmark. He also told me if I ever felt the urge to send another one, I should sublimate that urge in exercise, meditation, or suicide.

He admits to having received dozens of cards from women that range from the maudlin (baskets of pathetic kittens) to the downright sickening (Ziggy holding a "miss you" sign). He even discovered that if he wanted to get some woman to pay more attention to him, he'd simply not call her back and wait for the cute card to arrive.

Unfortunately, he also admits that as soon as this same woman stooped to the greeting card stage, he'd dislike her. It's a no-win situation and a blight on the face of this country. It's the hidden disease no one talks about.

## What to Do When the Hallmark Urge Hits

- Buy the sappiest card you can find and send it to someone you hate. At least you can get *him* to stop calling.

- Start a riot in the card store by laughing out loud at the religious cards.

- Hold up a Jesus card and ask the person next to you if it's a picture of Jesus or George Harrison.

- If you can't resist the urge to get *something* in the mail to him by the next post, send him a Spanish-language card and sign it Carlos. If, however, he *is* Spanish, send him a Ziggy card and sign it Carlos. He will go crazy and worry about his sexuality.

- Send him a condolence card for his birthday and sign it Carlos.

- Make a sign and put it over your bed that says: THE ONLY CARD WORTH ANYTHING IS PLASTIC.

- Throw yourself on the mercy of the clerk and beg her not to sell you anything.

- Form your own chapter of C.A.R.D. (Cards Are *Really* Desperate), and ask other women to share their humiliating card experiences. When the urge hits, you can call your C.A.R.D. "partner," and she'll talk you out of further humiliating yourself by sending it.

- Call your mother and blame it all on her.

## How to Not Make Hang-Up Calls
## When You Know He'll Know
## That It's You Acting Desperate

There is one more activity as humiliating as sending cute cards, and that's the hang-up call. Now, have you ever gotten a hang-up call and *not* known who it was?

It's bad enough that he will be sure that any *legit* hang-up call (when someone really *has* reached a wrong number and hangs up without speaking) is you, without you furthering the spread of the disease. Personally, I don't think there is such a thing as a legit hang-up call, but in all fairness I had to include it.

The subcategory of hang-up calls is the "I'll get my friend to call up and ask for someone else" call. Or in layman's terms, the fake wrong-number call. Now, excuse me, but what are you supposed to find out with these insane calls? Personally, I have never asked a friend to make one of these, but I sure have made them at 3:00 A.M. *for* crazed friends. The only reason I've never asked a friend to make one is because I was sure that the guy would know that I had coerced someone to make a wrong-number call. I am, obviously, extremely paranoid. Besides, all that I could find out from a call like that would be that:

A. He wasn't home, which would make me depressed.

B. He *was* home, which would make me depressed. (Because he wasn't, as I suspected, lying in some hospital, desperate to call me, but alas, paralyzed and unable to pick up the phone. This, incidentally, is the only legit reason for him not to call; all other reasons mean that he's not interested.)

C. He had a woman there (if one answered). From that I would conclude that they were engaged, which would make me depressed.

D. If a man answered his phone I would be sure that he was gay, which would make me depressed.

E. If his mother answered, I would have to kill myself, and reaffirm "D."

### What to Do Instead of Making Hang-Up Calls and Waiting by the Phone Like a Fat-Girl-Without-a-Date-for-the-Prom

- Take a walk . . . cross-country. It's healthy and you may meet Mr. Right at the Grand Canyon or when you go to get your shoes resoled in Philadelphia.

- Make hang-up calls to his parents' house at 3:00 A.M.

- Get out a Ouija board and call up dead relatives for advice.

- Go to a past-life therapist to find out if Mr. Wonderful was St. Anthony in a previous life and that's why he gets to be so cavalier in this one.

- Go to a past-life therapist to find out if you were Charles Manson, Goebbels, or Hitler in a previous life and that's why you have to be tormented in this one.

- Call your mother and blame it all on her.

- Call the phone company and blame it all on them.

- Go out and buy the *National Enquirer* or *The Weekly World News* and count the number of alien babies born in England last week. If you're lucky, they will have a story about someone who spontaneously exploded as well. Stories like these will always cheer you up. After all, you could be stuck with a glowing, bossy, alien baby right now, or even one of those children in Brazil who get old-age disease at three. It's enough to make you count your blessings! A subscription to one of these can keep you happy for the rest of your life. After all, what's a little misery when other people are spontaneously exploding?

# How to Avoid Turning Into
# a Big Nun

There is a subcategory of Fat Girl that is equally irritating, or maybe even more irritating. It's Big Nun behavior. Big Nun behavior stems from being abandoned and/or lied to by the man you craved.

Most women simply hire a paid killer to beat the man senseless and leave him for dead on the side of the road, which is reasonable. Martyr types (or Big Nuns) would never dream of having someone beaten senseless other than themselves. Therefore, since the situation desperately cries out for strict and unusual punishment, they punish themselves and save money to boot! (When you set out to do yourself in with Big Nun behavior, you needn't pay a soul . . . no pun intended).

## Know the Warning Signs!!!
## How to Tell if You Are Becoming a Big Nun

- You crave black lace-up shoes with thick heels.

- Instead of practicing come-hither wither looks, you stand in front of the mirror and say, "Get in line, no talking!"

- You have given your dog(s)/cat(s) children's names, like Jennifer or Anthony.

- Your conversation is beginning to center around the tricks Jenny and Tony can do.

- Your mother is no longer afraid to ask you to go to the church (synagogue, or whatever) bazaar with her.

- You're happy to go . . . it's a night out.

- The mothers of people your own age like you. A lot.

- When you go to buy a new car, you lean toward a light-blue Ford Fairlaine, with no trim, no radio, and plaid seats.

- You stop having vaginal infections from too much sex and too-tight jeans.

- You find yourself at a bar saying things like, "I'll have a nice cup of tea" instead of "Fill 'er up."

- The only strapless thing you own is a clutch purse.

## How to Escape Big Nun Living

The prospect of living like a Big Nun should be frightening enough for you to take serious action. Now, I'm not saying that you will be brave enough to follow all the suggestions outlined, but I hope you'll be sane enough to follow some of them.

- Change your animals' names immediately to something reasonable like Spot or Rin Tin Tin. Men hate women who have animals with kid names . . . it sounds pathetic.

- Seduce someone today.

- Go buy too-tight Wranglers.

- Buy six-inch spike heels and wear them to work with a black leather skirt.

- Invite a motorcycle gang over for drinks.

- Keep a riding crop at your desk. It makes you seem at best athletic and at worst, er, interesting.

- Send regrets to the rosary-saying competition.

- Learn to smoke, drink, and have runs in your hose.

- Give up white casseroles. Forever.

### Big Nuns Have Less Fun

Now in case you hadn't noticed, girls who display Big Nun Behavior have lots less fun than, say, blondes. While blondes are out stealing hub caps and other people's husbands, Big Nuns are doing something decent for someone else. While blondes are tearing the seams of too-tight skirts, Big Nuns are taking collections in the office for Mr. Burns's birthday/funeral/heart attack. Blondes don't even follow through on the contribution that they promised to give. Now, here's the kicker: Who is Mr. Burns going to come looking for at his birthday party/funeral/or hospital room? Not Big Nun, that's for sure! If that isn't enough to convince you to mend your ways, then nothing is!

### Remember: Nun Is Never Enough!

# How to Tell if Your Son Is Growing Up to Be an Impossible Man

Much has been written in recent years about the importance of discovering impossible-man traits in young men. Studies have been conducted, and the President's committee on the study of Impossible Men concluded that there is no such thing. The study was headed by Donald Regan *and* Oliver North.

In face of all of the evidence presented, I still step forward and present this list. Defy or deny if you like, but don't write me letters if that son of yours:

- Says things like, "I said lightly toasted, Mom . . . lightly toasted!" upon sitting down to breakfast. Every morning.

- Tries to divorce his sister.

- Is caught selling the big wooden key to the bathroom in nursery school.

- Worries that he might get cancer from Cocoa Krispies.

- Knows how to say *al dente* at age three. And means it.

- Asks the girls in camp if they brought a credit card.

- Wants to begin dating soon as he graduates from Pre-K.

- Says if you buy him designer jeans he will kill himself.

- Tries to pay off his sister's boyfriend to marry her and get her out of his hair. He's six, and the boy is twelve.

# Spotting a Really Impossible Man: Never Love a Man Who . . .

- Asks you how much you weigh, how much you used to weigh, and if you've ever thought of working out.
- Has hair spray in his bathroom that belongs to him.
- Has hair spray in his bathroom that doesn't belong to him.
- Clips coupons other than the ones attached to large stock portfolios.
- Can't fix a flat, beat up punks, or recite Chaucer. For you.
- Talks about his mother, his cat, or his ex-wife on your first date.
- Thinks that "supportive" means that the man works and the woman goes to PTA meetings and that "supporter" is something he wears when playing sports.
- Makes use of his blow dryer.
- Wears a gold bracelet.
- Gets manicured. A lot.
- Asks you to call him and then gives you his work number. Only.
- Takes forty words to express what can be said in three.
- Is not ashamed to have fur seats in his car.
- Owns a fur coat. And wears it.
- Owns a light-blue suit.

- Has never read the *National Enquirer* cover to cover, even once.

- Owns a pair of Italian gigolo shoes.

- Has a working relationship with his stereo, his computer, his car.

- Says "I'm something of a gourmet" before he sits down to dinner at *your* house.

- Says "I'm something of a gourmet" before you sit down to dinner at *his* house.

# Spotting a Possible Man: Always Love a Man Who . . .

**Y**es, there is such a thing. It's just that we're always so busy trying to nab a desperado that we only use the possibles to make the impossibles jealous. Or what's even worse, we use possibles to cry about impossibles to. Therefore:

*Always* Love a Man Who . . .

- Thinks you have great legs, no matter what *you* think.
- Knows that you are completely insane and neurotic but figures that nobody's perfect.
- Takes your kids ice skating without being asked.
- Gives you the keys to his car before you have an affair.
- Gives you the keys to his car after you've had an affair.
- Gives you his home phone number when he asks for yours.
- Buys you shoes.
- Owns a beach house.
- Buys *you* a beach house.
- Teaches your daughter how to steal home.
- Teaches three-year-olds how to play poker.
- Can make kids laugh. A lot.
- Can make you laugh. All the time.
- Knows that sex is the best way to have fun while laughing.
- Never has to say, "Was it good for you?" Ever.

# The Most Famous Phrases in Impossible-Man History

"I'll call you."

"There *is* no one else. I swear."

"After the next inning. I swear."

"It might seem like *only* a cold to *you*, but . . ."

"I'm working late."

"Gee, the switchboard must have gone dead, because I was there. I swear."

"Okay, so you caught me. I *do* put Chanel No. 5 on myself when I'm working late."

"Waiter, why is there a large piece of dried pecan pie on my fork?" (Dish, glass, napkin, cup, knife, spoon, etc.)

"Do you think I *want* to go to the Caribbean for two weeks without you? No! I'm forced to with this damn job!"

"Did you do the wash?"

"Did you do the wash with gray soap powder?

"Did you pick my shirts up from the Chinese laundry?"

"I said *extra* starch."

"What do you mean fifty-five long distance calls to the same number?"

"No! I'll call the phone company and straighten this mess out. Later. From my office."

"I don't care what the American Express bill says, I've never spent a weekend in Saint Moritz without you."

"No! I'll call American Express and straighten this mess out later. From my office."

# Famous Last Words:
## HIS

"I'll call you."

"There is no one else. I swear."

"I need some space."

"Put that gun away. You could hurt someone."

# Famous Last Words:
## YOURS

"I left your Ferrari on the freeway. It had a flat."

"I hear they're publishing a book of your poetry. It's called *I Wish I Hadn't Said That.*"

"Sorry to wake you this late, but that fish I made you for dinner seems to have been a lot older than I thought."

"Where did you learn to dance like that? Iraq?"

"Go fly a kite. Please."

"I'll call you. I swear."

"It's your mother on the phone."

"It's your wife on the phone."

"I don't care if Dallas is playing the *Pope.*"

"I can't marry you. I've got a Tupperware party to go to."

"It's not loaded."